# This Planet Is Mine

# This Planet Is Mine

*by Dianna Dee Damkoehler with Helen Gehrenbeck*

### SCHOLASTIC
# PROFESSIONAL BOOKS

NEW YORK • TORONTO • LONDON • AUCKLAND • SYDNEY

• • • • • • • • • • • • • • • • • • • • • • • • • • • • • • • • • • •

DEDICATION

*To my sons—Hans, Jason, and Aaron—who have*
*always filled my world with wonder,*
*and to the Earthkeeping children of Metcalf School,*
*my other family. I love you all!*
—D.D.D.

*To my family—David and our children, Robert, Mary Anne,*
*and Rick—for their encouragement and expertise;*
*and to all Metcalf School first-grade Earthkeepers and*
*their parents who make this book possible.*
—H.H.G.

Copyright © 1995 by Scholastic Inc.
Cover design by Vincent Ceci
Cover photo by Gerald Liebenstein
Interior design by Jacqueline Swensen
(Children's art used with permission)

0-590-48794-9

Printed in U.S.A.

Printed on recycled paper.                    12 11 10 9 8 7 6 5 4 3 2 1    4 5/9

# TABLE OF CONTENTS

# Goals for Earthkeepers

- Learn to observe well and see with "new eyes."

- Begin to sense that change is part of our lives and the planet's life.

- Understand that change can be fast or slow.

- Become aware of the cycles of the planet (day/night; seasons) and the cycles in nature.

- Come to sense the interdependence of living systems.

- Learn to ask good questions based on one's natural curiosity.

- Become familiar with instruments and techniques for recording observed Earth facts or expressing feelings.

- Be empowered to take responsible action and become life-long Earthkeepers.

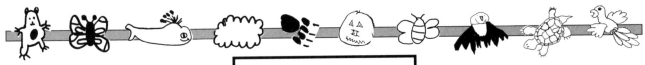

# INTRODUCTION: A Personal Note

The kids call me Mrs. Dee. I love children, the earth, good books, and magnificent teachers like Helen, so I relish the opportunity I have had to combine all these wonderful components into one dream project—developing an environmentally-focused and literature-based learning approach for young children. As Helen opened her mind and her classroom to my ideas our collaboration proved endlessly stimulating! I am an educational consultant with a deep interest in environmental education, and I have also been responsible for the primary level library program at school for almost a decade. Helen is a wonderful teacher with vast science and whole language expertise as well as a willingness to try something new. The book you are about to read is based on those experiences in a special classroom where anything was possible!

I believe that teachers are the most important and powerful creatures on the planet! Their influence can provoke wonder and provide wisdom—or it can close doors on curiosity forever in the mind and heart of a child. To accomplish the former is to perform a miracle. Good teachers do this a hundred time a day, and in the process bring great joy to their own lives and to the lives of the children they touch through their teaching.

One of the factors that contribute to a successful learning experience is the careful selection of "content vehicles." These are areas of study that a teacher explores with students in an effort to help them gain the necessary skills for living. The young child needs to learn to read, write, and gain ability in the manipulation of number processes. Children must have opportunities to practice these skills. The student also needs experience in the vital art of social interaction with peers and adults. The child is benefited by exposure to a variety of situations that will provide him/her with the opportunity to evaluate and make informed choices. These are difficult skills, but exciting things can happen if the child is interested in the area of study. A student will invest considerable energy in the pursuit of knowledge if spurred on by a natural relentless curiosity. If the process is well guided by a teacher, the child will not only absorb end-

less, valuable factual information, but he/she will also gain experience in using accumulated knowledge for critical thinking and decision-making. Teaching children about the importance and power of "choices" is perhaps one of the most significant tasks in education.

Which "content vehicles" does one choose for accomplishing all these ends? I once heard Jacques Cousteau say, "We take care of that which we love." I think we can extend this to say that we learn easily about that which we love. Children intrinsically care about the earth and all its creatures. Unless that natural curiosity is dulled by circumstances and influences beyond the child's control, it will prove the educator's greatest ally in motivating children to learn. A curriculum that pulls its "content vehicles" from the wondrous realms of the planet is sure to excite and intrigue children.

We have implemented this approach in *This Planet Is Mine.* For nine months our "content vehicles" have been selected to excite emerging Earthkeepers. Each area of study builds knowledge that enhances the next area of study. The excitement of the children grows along with their knowledge. Thread by thread, a tapestry of prior knowledge is woven and added to their store.

As we work our way through the various units in *This Planet is Mine* we follow a similar format. I always introduce the unit with an Earth Minute designed to stimulate curiosity and initiate discussion. We then include a Fact Box of interesting information. Literature Connections follow, highlighting special books on the subject area. Next we may explore various ways of integrating the idea through language arts, math, science, and social studies activities. We read and research the content area, always immersing the children in literature and hands-on experiences. We bring in special guests to enhance our knowledge. Soon it is time for Celebrations and feeling good about what we have learned. We take time for some World Wondering to consider how human actions and choices can affect our planet. We also encourage parent involvement by incorporating Family Tie activities.

The children learn that many problems are very complex. However, it is exciting to make good choices in an attempt to solve those problems. We celebrate the wonder of subject areas, considering the "earth connections" as we search for facts. A search for understanding that celebrates wonder and values wisdom is effective. By empowering the children to take positive actions in a variety of ways, difficult areas of study can be addressed without provoking fear, and indeed stimulating curiosity.

And so we have completed a wonderful year and can say from experience that children love the earth. Use that! They will learn more than you ever thought possible. Each child will become a fledgling Earthkeeper eager for her/his next discovery.

Enjoy the journey you take with your students, and remember the words of Rachel Carson, the author of *Silent Spring*: *"If I had influence with the good fairy who is supposed to preside over the christening of all children, I should ask that her gift to each child in the world be a sense of wonder so indestructable that it would last throughout life...."*

Dianna Dee Damkoehler

## NOTE TO THE CHILDREN

This year we are going to take a wonderful journey together that could be very exciting. Most of the time we will be right here in our classroom, but in our minds we will travel to the far corners of the Earth and into a drop of water and even under a leaf. We will explore many of the wonders of our planet on this journey, and I promise you will not believe the things to be discovered!

For the next year you all will be "Earthkeepers." To be good Earthkeepers you will need to learn to observe with the eyes of an Earth Watcher, for there are millions of things to see. Some things will be tiny, others huge, and most somewhere in between, but they all can be very interesting if one knows what to look for.

Together we will observe the creatures of the Earth and learn that sometimes you see more by touching with your eyes than with your hands.

You must also learn to listen with the ears of an Earth Listener, for sometimes her sounds are very loud, like thunder, but at other times they are as quiet as a falling leaf.

You will always be an Earth Detective, alert for any clues that could help us unravel a mystery.

There are many times when you will need to be an Earth Artist or an Earth Author, for there will probably be many things you will want to share with others, since the things you learn will be so interesting.

You might even be an Earth Speaker at times, as you talk about the Earth at school and home and almost anywhere. If you have learned something important or interesting it is good to share it with others, and that will also make you an Earth Teacher. This is going to be great fun, and so we begin!

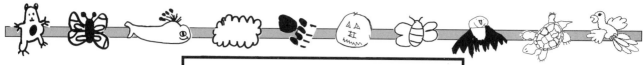

# SUGGESTIONS FOR EARTH

From the moment the children first come into the classroom they are celebrated as Earthkeepers! They enter an environment of beautiful green and blue colors. (Use fadeless bulletin board 48-inch paper rolls. The colors are soothing and last all year.) The room is filled with green plants and has a "natural" outdoors look about it. Baskets replace plastic containers when possible. An old tree stump serves as the teacher's place at a central carpet area. Various other logs and large branches adorn the room. These can be altered easily with the seasons. The large branch that drapes high over the reading table is secured there by inserting its trunk in the center hole of two stacked concrete blocks. (Tip: The best things are to be found on trash piles.) Dried prairie grasses create a prairie environment on a large shelf overlooking the room. (We haven't had a problem with allergies, but be aware of your students' needs!) A park bench is a reading area. Even the traditional numberline across the front board in the classroom is a continuous border strip depicting the planet earth. Use natural materials as frequently as possible for instructional manipulatives. For example, small pebbles can be used as counters. Rocks, birds' nests, shells, and many other items from nature accent various "Centers" in this environment. Supplement with selected posters, photos, and art.

1. **"This Planet is Mine" Job Assignment Board.** Individual earthkeeper tasks are logged here with a corresponding tag at the child's desk. Name tags were made by placing an earth sticker on a paper heart and nestling an animal sticker next to it.

2. **Earth Listener Center.** A listening center will be provided all year long with materials to appropriately enhance the areas of study.

3. **The Earthkeeper Center.** The content of this area will change all year long as well. It will hold books, posters, and supplemental manipulatives.

4. **The Aquarium.** This will remain on display all year long. A "Fish Observer Log" in which children are encouraged to write and illustrate personal observations is located there.

5. **Birdwatching Center.** This area is at a window with a prime outside view near the bird and squirrel feeders. A pair of binoculars is placed here along with a class Birdwatcher Log. Again, observation and entries are encouraged! Books particular to each area are always available for student browsing. The journals are created by having a child illustrate the cover with appropriate art. Then laminate and spiral bind entry papers that contain the heading, "I Observed."

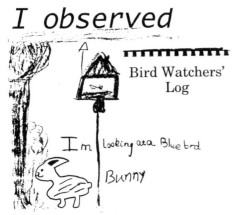

6. **Weather Center.** Thermometers and a rain guage are placed so children can easily observe them and record their findings.

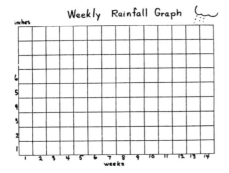

7. **Map and Globe Center.** Our location on the planet becomes real in the context of stories and projects. We put a small marker on a pull-down map to indicate where our various adventures had taken place.

8. **Classroom Animals.** THIS IS IMPORTANT! Animals are a wonderful addition to a classroom, but only under appropriate circumstances! We must teach interaction techniques. Good Earthkeepers often must learn to "Touch with your eyes and not with your hands!" Animals are living creatures, not dispensable classroom commodities. It is valuable for a child to learn how to observe quietly so as not to frighten and stress classroom creatures. We have taught our children nothing if we do not teach responsible interaction, kindness, and respect. We wrote a chant. "It's not cool to be cruel! (3X) That's the earth's golden rule! Yeah!"

9. **Final Note.** The physical environment of the room will remain natural all year long and will change as the earth changes. Children become alert Earth Observers and can record these changes.

# Suggestions for Earth Resources

## BOOKS ABOUT ANIMALS

**Chinery, Michael.** *Young World: All Kinds of Animals.* Random House, New York, 1993.

**Maynard, Christopher.** *Amazing Animal Facts.* Alfred A. Knopf, New York, 1993.

**Taylor, Barbara.** *The Animal Atlas.* Alfred A. Knopf, New York, 1992.

## BOOKS ABOUT BIRDS

**Arnosky, Jim.** *Crinkleroot's Guide to Knowing the Birds.* Bradbury, New York, 1992.

**Bash, Barbara.** *Urban Roosts:Where Birds Nest in the City.* Sierra Club, San Francisco, 1990.

**Jeunesse, Gallimard.** *Birds.* Scholastic, New York, 1990.

**Peterson, Roger Tory.** *First Guide to Birds.* Houghton Mifflin, Boston, 1986.

**Rockwell, Anne.** *Our Yard Is Full of Birds.* Macmillan, New York, 1992.

**Royston, Angela.** *Eye Openers: Birds.* Macmillan, New York, 1992.

**Sill, Cathryn.** *About Birds: A Guide for Children.* Peachtree, Atlanta, 1991.

## BOOKS ABOUT FISH

**Arnosky, Jim.** *Crinkleroot's 25 Fish Every Child Should Know.* Bradbury, New York, 1993.

**Evans, Mark.** *Fish: A Practical Guide to Caring for Your Fish.* ASPCA Pet Care Guide for Kids. Dorling Kindersley, New York, London, 1993.

**Wu, Norbert.** *Fish Faces.* Henry Holt, New York, 1993.

## BOOKS ABOUT RAIN

**Markle, Sandra.** *A Rainy Day.* Orchard Books, New York, 1993.

**Martin, Bill Jr.** *Listen to the Rain.* Henry Holt, New York, 1988.

**Polacco, Patricia.** *Thunder Cake.* Putnam, New York, 1990.

**Serfozo, Mary.** *Rain Talk.* Scholastic, New York, 1990.

**Turner, Ann.** *Rainflowers.* HarperCollins, New York, 1992.

## BOOKS ABOUT SQUIRRELS

**Bare, Colleen Stanley.** *Busy, Busy Squirrels.* Dutton, New York, 1991.

**Ehlert, Lois.** *Nuts to You.* HBJ, San Diego, 1993.

**Miller, Edna.** *Scamper: A Gray Tree Squirrel.* Pippin Press, New York, 1991.

**Ryden, Hope.** *The Raggedy Red Squirrel.* Dutton, New York, 1992.

## BOOKS ABOUT LOOKING AND LISTENING

**Albert, Richard E.** *Alejandro's Gift.* Chronicle Books, San Francisco, 1994.

**Borden, Louise.** *The Watching Game.* Scholastic, New York, 1991.

**Collins, Pat Lowery.** *I Am an Artist.* Millbrook, Brookfield, Connecticut, 1992.

**Day, David.** *Aska'a Animals.* Doubleday, Toronto, Ontario, 1991.

**Noll, Sally.** *Lucky Morning.* Greenwillow, New York, 1994.

**Pearce, Q.L.,** and **W. J. Pearce.** *Nature's Footprints: In the Forest.* Silver Press, Englewood Cliffs, New Jersey, 1990.

**Ryder Joanne.** *Under Your Feet.* Four Winds, New York, 1990.

**Selsam, Millicent.** *Keep Looking.*
Macmillan, New York, 1989.

**Williams, David.** *Walking to the Creek.*
Alfred A. Knopf, New York, 1993.

## "EARTHKEEPER" ART

**Kohl, Mary Ann F.,** and **Cindy Gainer.**
*Good Earth Art: Environmental Art for
Kids.* Bright Ring, Bellingham,
Washington, 1991.

**Owen, Cheryl.** *My Nature Craft Book.*
Little, Brown, Boston, 1993.

## POETRY CONNECTION

**Adoff, Arnold,** and **Jerry Pinkney.** *In for
Winter, Out for Spring.* HBJ, San Diego,
1991.

**Brenner, Barbara, Ed.** *The Earth Is
Painted Green: A Garden of Poems
About Our Planet.* Scholastic, New York,
1994.

**de Regniers, Beatrice Schenk.** *Sing A
Song of Popcorn: Every Child's Book of
Poems.* Scholastic, New York, 1988.

**Lewis, J. Patrick.** *Earth Verses and Water
Rhymes.* Atheneum, New York, 1991.

**Marsh, James.** *Bizarre Birds and Beasts.*
Dial, New York, 1991.

**Moore, Lilian.** *Sunflakes: Poems for
Children.* Clarion, New York, 1992.

**Nature, Mother.** *Mother Nature Nursery
Rhymes.* Advocacy, Santa Barbara,
California, 1990.

**Paladino, Catherine.** *Land, Sea and Sky:
Poems to Celebrate the Earth.* Little,
Brown, Boston, 1993.

**Prelutsky, Jack.** *The Random House Book
of Poetry for Children: A Treasury of
572 Poems for Today's Child.* Random
House, New York, 1983.

**Sheeham, William.** *Nature's Wonderful
World in Rhyme.* Advocacy, Santa
Barbara, 1993.

**Yolen, Jane.** *Bird Watch: A Book of Poetry.*
Philomel, New York, 1990.

## EARTH ALPHABET BOOKS

**Berg, Camil.** *D is for Dolphin.* Windom
Books, Santa Fe, New Mexico, 1992.

**Fain, Kathleen.** *Handsigns: A Sign
Language Alphabet.* Chronicle Books,
San Francisco, 1993.

**Feldman, Judy.** *The Alphabet in Nature.*
Children's Press, Chicago, 1991.

**McPhail, David.** *Animals A to Z.*
Scholastic, New York, 1988.

**Mullins, Pat.** *V for Vanishing.*
HarperCollins, New York, 1994.

**Twinem, Neecy.** *Aye-ayes, Bears and
Condors.* Freeman, New York, 1994.

## EARTH COUNTING BOOKS

**Clements, Andrew.** *Mother Earth's
Counting Book.* Picture Book Studio,
Saxonville, Massachusetts, 1992.

**Morozumi, Atsuko.** *One Gorilla.* Farrar,
Straus and Giroux, New York, 1990.

**Owens, Mary Beth.** *Counting Cranes.*
Little, Brown, Boston, 1993.

**Wallwork, Amanda.** *No Dodos,* Scholastic,
New York, 1993.

# My Home on the Prairie

*"The prairie sings to me in the*
*forenoon and I know in the night*
*I rest easy in the prairie arms,*
*on the prairie heart."*

—Carl Sandburg

### The Journey Begins at Home... Wherever That May Be!

We live in Illinois, the heart of what was once a vast and wondrous sea of grass called the tallgrass prairie, but most children in our state have never seen prairie grass. We are nicknamed the "Prairie State" and yet remain unaware of our extraordinary heritage. Through special guests and a good selection of books, we go back in time to our roots in the prairie. We research, listen, and learn. You can adapt these suggestions to *your* region:

- **Parents are history books!** Children were sent home with a note and questions to ask their parents. What did they know about the prairie? Did any of their ancestors live in Illinois? What was it like then? Are there any old family pictures that might provide clues as to what life

I know that summer
        has begun.
The  monarch flitters
        in the sun.
The colors are always
        shining in the sky.
And she flutters past me
        by and by.
I am sitting on a pile
        of hay.
Just watching the day
    flutter away.

was like long ago? Perhaps some parents might come to school and share pictures and stories of those early prairie times in their family history.

- **Books about prairies past and present.** We read a great story called *Lottie's Dream* by Bonnie Pryor (Simon and Schuster, 1992) about a little girl who grew up on the early prairies. We tried to imagine what it would have been like to live then. We thought about following a beautiful monarch through grasses so tall that children had to be tied together when walking so they could not become lost! We drew wordless stories imagining our life on the prairie. One child wrote a poem about watching the monarch long ago. We also looked at a beautiful book called *A Sea of Grass: The Tallgrass Prairie* by David Dvorak, Jr. (Macmillan, New York, 1994). We saw all kinds of beautiful pictures of plants and animals of the prairie, but we noticed it didn't look much like that near our homes anymore. The buffalo were gone, along with the tall grasses. We learned that less than 1% of the original prairie still remains! We knew that one part left out of a hundred parts was not very much left. We looked at the prairie grasses in the classroom and wanted to see what it was like 100 years ago.

- **A prairie expert.** A man who loved the prairie came to talk to us about it and its inhabitants. We were learning as Earthkeepers to be curious about many new things. We really hadn't thought much about our prairie home before. He told us about the plants and animals living there.

- **A prairie field trip!** We are lucky to have a little piece of prairie not far from school so we went to see it. It was beautiful and we were sorry so much of it was gone. We learned that it was "endangered." This means that if it is not "protected," someday soon there might not be any more prairie. That would be sad. We loved our field trip to the prairie! We saw how tall the grasses were and we could hear the swish of the wind through them, just as children of long ago might have heard. We sat on a blanket in the middle of our ancient home and read *Where Are My Prairie Dogs and Black Footed Ferrets?* by Ron Hirschi (Bantam Books, 1992).

- **Prairie wondering.** Where have all the prairies gone? As we drove back on our field trip we passed many cornfields, but maybe it is time to save a little for the prairie and its creatures! We were getting very curious about a place we had not even thought about before.

- **Discussing "change."** The prairies had really changed over time. As Earthkeepers we were going to be watching for "change" and recording many kinds of changes. It was an easy time to start thinking about changes and what they mean.

## The Journey Continues....

We are children of the prairie, so we begin our earth year celebrating these majestic "seas of grass" as we prepare to reach out to the other marvelous places on the planet during our Earthkeeper adventures of the coming year. However, you and your students might be children of the mountains, deserts, wetlands, or cities! Begin where you are on the earth. Celebrate your roots, then join us on our journey!

# For the Love of Monarchs

*"The butterfly counts not months but moments, and has time enough."*

—Rabin-Dranath Tagore (1928)

Fragile and majestic, a tiny orange and black butterfly has enchanted our hearts for centuries. Our monarch study initiates an exploration into the intriguing interconnectedness of all living creatures and ecosystems. No animal on earth can better capture our imagination than the incredible monarch butterfly! Through the systematic investigation of this creature's life cycle much can be learned about the monarch and about scientific processes. Our first Animal of the Month is to be this amazing butterfly!

## Earth Minute:
### I Wish I Were a Butterfly

One beautiful late summer day, I came softly into the room draped in a flowing orange cloth and wearing a long black skirt wistfully repeating the phrase, "I wish I were a butterfly." I floated over to the story stump, then shared the visually stunning book, *I Wish I Were a Butterfly* by James Howe (Gulliver Books, 1987). As I read the book the children empathized with the plaintive and repeated cry of the little cricket as he called out "Oh I wish I were a butterfly!" After the story we talked about butterflies and remembered we had found monarch eggs on the milkweed plant. It seemed time to investigate one of nature's most incredible circles—the life cycle of the butterfly. Thus began our wondrous Butterfly Earthwatch!

## Literature Connections:
### Teaching with Books about Butterflies

#### READING A BUTTERFLY TALE

On another golden fall day we sat outside the classroom under a tree and read *The Lamb and the Butterfly* by Arnold Sundgaard (Orchard Books, 1988). In this story a curious lamb follows the path of a daring butterfly. The lamb ultimately learns why the creature cannot stay with him.

- **Butterfly questions.** We began to share what we knew about butterflies. Like the lamb in the story, we were full of questions!

  Where can we find monarchs?
  What do they eat?
  How are they born?
  How long does it
      take to become
      a butterfly?
  Where do they go
      when it's cold?

- **A silent observation walk.** We wanted to investigate these lovely creatures and find out more about their lives. "They are so quiet!" one student said. We decided to take a "Silent Butterfly Walk" and see what we could observe about monarchs around our school. We moved as silently as the butterfly as we set off in search of telltale monarch signs. We came back to the classroom after our "flight" and began our monarch Journals.

## A Folk Tale of Butterfly Wisdom

Another exquisitely illustrated book, *Darkness and the Butterfly*, by Ann Grifalconi (Little, Brown and Company, 1987) gently relates the African tale of Osa, a young child who is terrified of darkness. She confides in the Wise Woman that she is so small she fears she could not outrun the frightening creatures in her dreams. The woman comforts her saying that a much smaller creature—the butterfly—finds its way in the darkness. Osa dreams of the yellow butterfly and ultimately finds her own wings as the butterfly teaches her how to carry her own light.

- **Writing our version.** After reading the story we created our own books retelling the tale. The results were magical!

- **Creating a "Dark Butterfly Bulletin Board."** On a black paper background,

## *Did You Know?* MONARCH FACTS

○ All butterflies belong to the animal kingdom.

○ Butterflies are cold-blooded. They are the same temperature as the air around them.

○ A monarch usually lays only one egg on the underside of a leaf of a milkweed plant.

○ In two weeks, a monarch caterpillar multiplies its original weight by 2,700 times. (If a baby weighed six pounds at birth, it would weigh eight tons at the age of two weeks.)

○ Butterflies taste with their feet.

○ The male monarch is identified by a black spot on each of its rear wings.

○ Butterflies use their proboscises (thin straw-like tubes) to drink nectar.

○ Orange and black are nature's warning colors, so the monarch's bright colors warn predators that they might be poisonous.

○ The monarch flies as high as 2,000 feet and migrates up to 4,000 miles.

○ The monarch's antennae help to keep its balance in flight.

○ Monarchs winter in Mexico and California, but in the summer they live all over the continent.

○ Monarchs are the only butterflies in the world known to migrate.

○ The monarch's habitat is endangered when forests are cut down. They are threatened when milkweed is destroyed by farmers and gardeners using pesticides.

we attached brightly colored "dream butterflies" and other "gentle creatures of the night." We also attached notes to tell how we felt about the wise butterflies. "Black Beauty is kind," wrote Sarah. Some of us named our butterflies.

# Integrating the Idea:

## LANGUAGE ARTS: The Butterfly Jar Experience

A jar with a silk butterfly closed in it was on Helen's desk. She read the poem, *The Butterfly Jar* by Jeff Moss (Bantam Books, 1989). It was beautiful. It spoke of the dreams and wonderings that can be locked inside us until somehow they are set free! She opened the jar and gently removed the butterfly and said, "Now it is free." She and the children talked about what "freedom" means. What did it mean to the butterfly? They drew a picture of the butterfly at the moment of its freedom and imagined and wrote its thoughts!

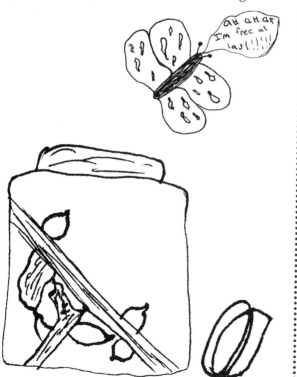

## LANGUAGE ARTS: A "Buggy" Poetry Break

I came into the room carrying a silver bug attached to a small branch. I shouted "Poetry Break!" and recited the poem, "A Bug Sat in a Silver Flower" by Karla Kuskin. We loved this poem about a bug who is eaten along with his underwear! It began a "For the Love of Bugs" poetry break. Then we created our own bug and butterfly poems. We memorized lots of butterfly poems like "The Caterpillar" by Christina Rosetti.

## SCIENCE/MATH: Metamorphosis Magic

We had become intensely interested in butterflies, and everyone was eager to learn more about them, so we charted our course.

- **Predictions and reality.** We predicted how long it would take to "grow" a butterfly, then we read *When Will You Be a Butterfly* by Elva Robinson and saw the photographs of each of the stages. Incredible!

- **Names and stages.** We learned the names of the stages and drew, sequenced, and labeled these four stages on construction paper: the egg, caterpillar (larva), pupa (chrysalis), and butterfly (adult). We compared our stages with those in a beautiful book, *Butterflies: See How They Grow* (Dorling Kindersley,1988).

- **Classroom chart.** We made a classroom chart, "Facts We Have Learned About the monarch."

- **Monarch fact tree.** We created a monarch Tree after we read that monarchs migrate and hang by the hundreds in trees. Each time we learned a new fact, we cut out a monarch and wrote the new fact on the back and hung it on our tree. Our tree filled with monarchs, our heads filled with knowledge, and our hearts filled with wonder!

- **Interview with an expert.** We interviewed a guest expert who had tracked and photographed the monarch for years. She said, "You never get too old to love butterflies and you can never start too young to learn about them."

- **Monarch parts.** We became fascinated with the parts of a butterfly, and some of us made drawings of these incredible creatures.

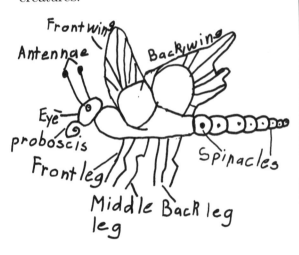

- **Gathering eggs.** We gathered eggs from the milkweed plants in our school garden. We took home information to share with parents about how and where to find monarch eggs. One father came in with monarch eggs and a tale of his family search for them. The wonder was widening! (If you are unable to collect eggs you can write to Lore Products for a Painted Lady Butterfly Kit.)

- **Microscopic wonders.** We carefully placed an egg on a leaf under a microscope and we could see a tiny creature inside. It was incredible!

- **A monarch center.** We created a monarch Center with all kinds of books, posters, and our large bug aquarium. We placed our monarch eggs and caterpillars in the aquarium and made sure we had fresh milkweed for them to eat each day. We covered it with wire screen in hopes that the caterpillar would spin the chrysalis from this top. And then the wait was on!

*Today is Sept. 20, 1993*
*I fond 2 Monarch eggs!*

- **The miracle is complete!** At long last the patient Earthwatchers are rewarded! On the eighteenth day, by our chart, the miracle occurred. As we watched, the chrysalis hanging from the top of the aquarium moved and the living creature worked its way through yet another of nature's complex and marvelous cycles. Over the next few days we observed much that was amazing!

  Observed the caterpillar's movements eating and shedding.

  Measured the graph and length of each caterpillar daily.

**21**

Counted how many milkweed leaves the caterpillar eats.

Observed tiny changes in the chrysalis.

Observed the emergence from the chrysalis, watching in awe how the limp creature struggles to pump its wings.

We have become witnesses to the wonder of metamorphosis and will remember it all our lives.

The Butterfly

I saw a Caterpillar hatch.
It was in a milk weed patch.
It crawled on a leaf
   that was Shaped like a peach
It shed its skin and was
     narrow as a pin
It made a bed
   on the very first try

then became a
   Butterfly!

## SCIENCE/MATH:
## Monarch Treat

While we waited and watched, we charted our monarch's daily progress in our monarch Logs. We studied the twelve segments of the caterpillar's body and created delicious segmented delicacies out of marshmallows and fruit segments. As we enjoyed eating our creations, Helen read *The Very Hungry Caterpillar* by Eric Carle (Putnam Publishers, 1981).

## SOCIAL STUDIES:
## Butterflies of Long Ago

Now that our long vigil had been rewarded with our wonderful butterfly we wondered if children of long ago had watched

monarchs. Some Native American legends talk about how butterflies came to be. In one, the Great Spirit hides lovely stones in the mountains so that people will love the mountains. But they are so beautiful he decides not to hide them and allows the south wind to carry them as living things for people to love. In another legend found in *Keeper of the Animals* by Michael J. Caduto and Joseph Bruchac (Fulcrum Publishers, Golden, Colorado, 1991), the butterflies at first can sing, but the Great Spirit realizes that song belongs to the birds. After our talk of legends, we each were presented with a small colored stone. We created a story about our own personal Earth Butterfly!

● **More butterfly history.** Another beautiful history lesson in butterflies can be found in *The Butterflies Come* by Leo Politi (Charles Scribner's Sons, 1957). This old story celebrates the monarch's return to Pacific Grove, California, a phenomenon that has taken place for centuries! This story can serve as an introduction to the next monarch wonder—migration!

## SOCIAL STUDIES:
## Butterfly Maps and Messages

We located our own place on the planet. Then we located California and placed an arrow on the path the butterflies might have taken to get there. We learned butterflies live everywhere on the planet except the north and south poles!

● **Migration Day Festival.** We wrote to Pacific Grove, California, to learn about their Migration Days Festival on February 11. They honor not only the return of the monarch, but also the migration of the gray whale and other animals.

● **Letters to our monarch.** We wrote letters to our "Midwestern monarch" and mailed them to Pacific Grove. These letters were displayed in California long after our monarchs had migrated from the prairie!

- **A city "monarch vote."** We learned the property in Pacific Grove, to which some monarchs migrate, was scheduled to be sold to developers. Many citizens did not want the monarchs to lose their homes. A vote was scheduled to see if the citizens would give money to buy the property. How would you vote? We held a classroom vote. It was unanimous for the monarch!

- **National Insect nomination.** We wrote letters asking our representatives to make the monarch our National Insect. (It is already the State of Illinois Insect.)

# Celebrations:

## A Monarch March

We had learned so much from our observation of our orange and black friends. We could even tell a male butterfly from a female

by the spots on the wings. But now it was time to get ready to say good-bye, and we planned to do so in style!

- **A monarch song.** We wrote a song for the monarchs called the "Monarch March."

- **A monarch march.** We planned a monarch March and migration across the school grounds, just as our butterflies would begin their migration.

- **Monarch costumes.** We made costumes for fun to represent the four stages of the monarch. We all got to wear antennae made by attaching yellow puffs to black pipe stems and securing them to headbands!

- **Monarch flag.** We made a monarch Flag and signs that told people how we felt about the monarch.

- **The march.** And so we marched, antennae bobbing in the breeze, and sang our song! We were Earth Speakers for our beloved monarch!

- **Nectar in the classroom.** After our march, we migrated back to the room where we sipped nectar and ate monarch-shaped cake treats!

### THE MONARCH MARCH
by First Graders
#### Stanza 1
First we started out as an egg one day
Next the larva stage and we ate all
the way;
Then we changed to a pupa, then a
butter...fly.
We're the Monarch Butterflies!
#### Chorus
We're the Monarch Butterflies!
We're the Monarch Butterflies!
We're the Monarch Butterflies!
We're the Monarch Butter. . flies!
#### Stanza 2
Now we're migrating to the south, you
know,

**23**

To California and Mexico;
We'll be back some . . day, from far
    a .. way.
We're the Monarch Butterflies!
**Chorus** (Repeat)
**Stanza 3**
    Some places people cut down our
    homes,
    And if they do, we'll no longer roam.
    But if people just care
    We will always be there.
    There'll be Monarchs everywhere!

# World Wondering:
## Butterfly Good-byes

### A FAREWELL STORY

We gathered at the story stump, and Helen placed the monarch aquarium on the floor at the center of the circle. We were excited and a little sad because we knew it was almost time to say good-bye. I read *The Butterfly Hunt* by Yoshi (Picture Book Studio, 1990). In this story a child works hard to capture a beautiful butterfly in his net. He does so and then realizes he must let it go, for the freedom he was taking from the butterfly was not really his to take. He sets his captive free!

And so did we. We remembered the wise words, "If you love something, set it free. If it comes back to you, it is yours. If it doesn't, it never was."

### A LAST GOOD-BYE

We took our monarch outside and with high spirits watched her lift her wings and sail on the currents high into the golden sky. We all wished our butterfly a safe journey and wondered how long the trip would take. The children will never forget this butterfly and all they had learned from her. We were glad to know that in Pacific Grove there is a $1,000 fine for harming a monarch. We all sensed in that moment that we were part of a tiny miracle!

# Family Tie:
## Monarch Magic Afternoon

The children wanted to share what we had learned with their parents, so we made plans.

- **Butterfly invitations to parents.** We made butterfly notes inviting parents to be our "Prairie Partners" at our monarch Magic Afternoon.

- **Sharing the facts.** Parents and friends visited our monarch Center, and we shared all our logs and charts and stories and poems.

- **Partners in the garden.** We read together *Where Butterflies Grow* by Joanne Ryder (Lodestar, 1989). We imagined that we had been transformed into butterflies and were a part of all the other creatures in a lovely garden. The children "partnered" with their parents (this could be done with another grade level, also), took clipboards with research guides attached out to our school garden, and worked together. It was fun! We made a leaf rubbing of a plant from the garden-home of our butterfly.

- **A video to remember.** We returned to the classroom and shared the documentary video, *In Honor of the Monarch Butterfly* from the Xerxes Society. It showed the phases of metamorphosis. We would remember this unit always!

# Books about Butterflies

**Butterfield, Moira.** *Butterfly.* Simon and Shuster Tenny, New York, 1991.

**DeLuise, Dom.** *Charlie the Caterpillar.* Simon and Shuster, New York, 1990.

**Drew, David.** *Caterpillar Diary.* Rigby Education, Crystal Lake, Illinois, 1988.

**Florian, Douglas.** *Discovering Butterflies.* Aladdin Books, New York, 1986.

**Garlick, May.** *Where Does theButterfly Go When it Rains?* Young, Scott, New York, 1989.

**Gibbons, Gail.** *Monarch Butterfly.* Holiday House, New York, 1989.

**Grifalconi, Ann.** *Darkness and the Butterfly.* Little, Brown and Co., Boston, 1987.

**Harvey, Diane Kelsay and Bob Harvey.** *Melody's Mystery, El Misterio De Melodia.* Beautiful American, Wilsonville, Oregon, 1991.

**Heller, Ruth.** *How to Hide a Butterfly.* Platt and Munk, New York, 1992.

**Howe, James.** *I Wish I Were a Butterfly.* Gulliver Books, New York, 1987.

**Julivert, Angels.** *Butterfly and Moths.* Barron's Educational Series, New York, 1991.

**Lasky, Kathryn.** *Monarch.* Harcourt Brace, New York, 1994.

**Lavies, Bianca.** *Monarch Butterflies: Mysterious Travelers.* Dutton, New York, 1992.

**Ling, Mary.** *Butterfly.* Dorling, New York, 1992.

**Marr, Molly.** *I Wonder Where Butterflies Go in Winter.* Western, New York, 1992.

**Paulus, Trina.** *Hope for the Flowers.* Newman, New York, 1972.

**Politi, Leo.** *The Butterflies Come.* Charles Scribner's Sons, New York, 1957.

**Robinson, Elva.** *When Will You Be a Butterfly?* DLM Teaching Resources, Allen, Texas, 1989.

**Ryder, Joanne.** *Where Butterflies Grow.* Lodestar Books, New York, 1989.

**Still, John.** *Amazing Butterflies and Moths.* Alfred A. Knopf, New York, 1991.

**Sundgaard, Arnold.** *The Lamb and the Butterfly.* Orchard Books, New York, 1988.

**Taylor, Kim.** *Butterfly: See How They Grow Series.* Dorling Kindersley, New York, 1988.

**Yoshi.** *The Butterfly Hunt.* Picture Book Studio, Saxonville, Massachusetts, 1990.

## AUDIOVISUAL MATERIALS

*Butterflies* (VHS). Coca-Cola Foundation (Contact the Education Department, Callaway Gardens, Pine Mountain, Georgia 31822, (404) 663-5153.)

NOTE: source for ordering Live Butterfly Raising Kits: Insect Lore Products, P.O. Box 1535, Shafter, California 93263, (805) 746-6047.

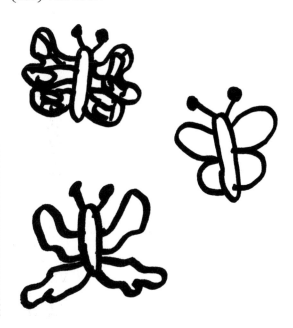

# The Changing Earth— Autumn

*"Go for a walk in the woods and remember to keep looking up,*
*around and down...If you hurry by, you will miss a lot.*
*Where there are old stumps and fallen branches,*
*stop and scan, slowly. Nature doesn't reveal all her secrets at once."*

—Elizabeth Terwillger

There is a different feel to the earth these days. The air is a bit chilly all of a sudden and a sweater begins to be comfortable! Then one magical day the air is filled with distant honking sounds, and we peer eagerly upward into the sky in the hope of catching a glimpse of the ancient V-shaped migration pattern of wild geese. The season has begun to change, and of all the earth's patterns and cycles this must be among the most exciting. Children love observing the changes in the earth's patterns that signal the autumn. An endless variety of changes can now be observed, written about, drawn and documented... as we learn to look and listen with the eyes and ears of an Earthkeeper! Each discovery is cause for celebration. This is the time for leaf walks and saying good-bye to summer as we watch the color come into the leaves and then see them fall.

## We Took a Fall Fieldtrip to a Pumpkin Farm

- **A search for signs.** We set off through the golden autumn in search of signs of the season. We used all of our senses to discover signs of change. Our Earthkeeper eyes could see quickly the new colors of the earth and our skin could feel the chill. We observed the changes in the grass around the small pond. Most of it was now brown.

- **A Fall poem.** The poetry of fall can be heard in the gentle wind if one listens with Earthkeeper ears! We could hear it rustle the dry grass and the leaves. Before we left the woods we took a clipboard to write a poem. It felt like a poem here!

## Pumpkin Wondering

- **A Pumpkin ecology tale.** While at the farm, we saw a field like the one in *Pumpkins*, a story by Mary Lyn Ray. In the story the man loved a pumpkin field and  it was going to be destroyed. He figured out a way to save his pumpkins. We talked about how that can happen in the real world and how we need to learn to make good choices. We can have what we need and still take care of the earth. That's being a good Earthkeeper.

## The Life of Leaves

- **Learning from a leaf.** We saw huge trees at the pumpkin farm and took some of their leaves back to school. We learned about the changes that happen to leaves in fall, and about chloroplasts, which are like tiny packages inside the cells of the leaf that are filled with colors. We learned how the sun and air and water are important to the leaf. Each leaf is like a little factory using the power of the sun to produce food for the plant. All summer the leaves have been making sugar, which is the plant's food. When the fall comes there are exciting reasons why this stops happening and the leaves begin to change color.

- **Classifying types of leaves.** As we studied the leaves we observed, compared and classified differences in their colors and shapes. We were excited by all the different types we found. We learned about simple and compound leaves, and we pressed them and made leaf rubbings. There is a lot to be looked at when looking at leaves! We noticed how some of the leaves in pictures in our books had been damaged by pollution in the air and water. We thought we would like to learn more about how that can happen.

## "Earth-Change" Art

- **A guest artist.** A guest artist visited the room and read us a story about autumn. We talked about all the changes that were happening. She told us she loved to watch the earth change. She asked us to choose one tree to watch and report its changes during the entire school year. She showed us how to use sponges to create the look of the tree in fall. We also drew our tree in winter. She promised to come back in the spring and show us neat ways to draw our spring and summer trees. We would

fall is the time for leves
fall is the time for fun.
I nevr wont
fall to go a way. but I
how at will but at will kymban

have to be good earth observers so that we could remember all the changes to discuss with her during our "tree talk" session. It is good to be able to recall earth facts for a long time, because some changes don't happen fast at all!

## More Autumn Art...

**Corn husks creativity.** Jonathan's mom came and brought Indian cornstalks. They were very tall. We measured them and put them up in the corner of the classroom. It made it feel like the fall was coming into the room. We used some of the corn husks to make cornhusk dolls. Our classroom continued to change with the changing season!

## LEAF WONDERING: Where Do They Go?

The leaves had really begun to fall now and were gathering deep on the ground. We wondered what happens to them all. Some are burned, it was suggested, but as Earth-keepers we wondered if that was really good for the air or for us. One child with asthma told us how she had to remain inside the house when she went to visit her grandmother in a town that allowed people to burn leaves. We called the mayor to find out the rules about burning leaves in our town. He told us there were rules against it because it

wasn't good for the air we all needed to breathe. We began to wonder what the earth did with her leaves if she was left alone. One child said his mom covered her plants with them for the winter to keep them warm. We continued to wonder and brainstorm.

- **Boot soup: An Experiment in Compost.** I read a story, *The Boot,* by Chris Baines (Crocodile, New York, 1990). It was an interesting tale of an old boot that is left behind on the ground for a long time. A variety of creatures dig in and make it home. Will the boot ever rot away? What happens to the leaves?

  We decided to take an old aquarium and fill it with some dirt, leaves, and an old boot. We thought we would throw in a few worms, then wait and see what might happen to our "boot soup." We also put some other objects in our boot soup to see if the earth would "take them back." We watched and recorded no progress for several days. Then we decided if anything was going to happen it would probably take more time, so we sat our boot aquarium outside the classroom door, behind the bushes where the rain or snow could add their influence.

  We each made our predictions about the outcome and then went on to other journeys. We had begun to think that this change in nature might take some time! And maybe there would be no change at all. We would simply have to be patient Earthwatchers and wait to see.

See p. 101

# Books about Autumn

## BOOKS ABOUT PUMPKINS

**Cuyler, Margery.** *The All Around Pumpkin Book.* Holt, Rinehart, Winston, New York, 1980.

**Hall, Zoe.** *Pumpkin Time.* Blue Sky/Scholastic, New York, 1994.

**King, Elizabeth.** *The Pumpkin Patch.* Dutton Children's Books, New York, 1990.

**McDonald, Megan.** *The Great Pumpkin Switch.* Orchard, New York, 1992.

**Miller, Edna.** *Mousekin's Golden House.* Prentice-Hall, Englewood Cliffs, New Jersey, 1964.

**Ray, Mary Lynch.** *Pumpkins.* Harcourt Brace Jovanovich, New York, 1992.

**Titherington, Jeanne.** *Pumpkin Pumpkin.* Scholastic, New York, 1986.

## BOOKS ABOUT AUTUMN

**Carlstrom, Nancy White.** *Goodbye Geese.* Philomel, New York, 1991.

**Ewart, Claire.** *One Cold Night.* G. P. Putnam's Sons, New York, 1992.

**Good, Elaine W.** *Fall Is Here! I Love It!* Good Books, Intercourse, Pennsylvania, 1990.

**Hirschi, Ron.** *Fall.* Cobblehill, New York, 1990.

**Kellogg, Steven.** *Johnny Appleseed: A Tale Retold.* Morrow Junior, New York, 1988.

**Knutson, Kimberley.** *Ska-tat!* Macmillan, New York, 1993.

**Maestro, Betsy.** *Why Do Leaves Change Color?* HarperCollins, New York, 1994.

**Markle, Sandra.** *Exploring Autumn, A Season of Science Activities, Puzzles, and Games.* Antheneum, New York, 1991.

**Micucci, Charles.** *The Life and Times of the Apple.* Orchard, New York, 1992.

**Ryder, Joanne.** *Chipmunk Song.* E. P. Dutton, New York, 1987.

**Schweninger, Ann.** *Autumn Days.* Viking Penguin, New York, 1991.

## BOOKS ABOUT LEAVES

**Beame, Rona.** *Leaf Collecting Album.* Workman, New York, 1989.

**Ehlert, Lois.** *Red Leaf, Yellow Leaf.* Harcourt Brace Jovanovich, New York, 1991.

**Lyon, George Ella.** *ABCedar, An Alphabet of Trees.* Orchard, New York, 1989.

**Sohi, Morteza.** *Look What I Did with a Leaf!* Walker, New York, 1993.

**Speed, Toby.** *One Leaf Fell.* Stewart, Tabori, & Chang, New York, 1993.

# The Wonder of Water

*"If there is magic on Earth it is contained in water.*
*Only water possesses the power to dissolve a mountain,*
*the artistry to paint the sky, and the strength*
*to support the great whale!"*

—Loren Eiseley

## An Aquarium Mystery

For several days the children peered into the thirty-gallon aquarium in a diligent effort to be good earth observers and report what they had seen, yet try as they might they could not catch sight of any elusive aquatic creatures. In fact, we had not yet placed the fish in the water for we were waiting for the conditions to be correct. The children, unaware of this, continued to construct elaborate theories as to the nature of the life they suspected was in the tank. Some even wrote in their observation logs where they felt the water creatures were hiding and why. Two drew pictures indicating what they suspected the creatures looked like. Endless interesting discussion and theorizing took place! They were amused and delighted when at long last several plastic bags containing real fish were observed floating in the tank waiting for the temperature to equalize! They joyfully shared their feelings that they were certain something was there in the tank, and there actually wasn't! We talked about how there may be times we think something is true that

is not true. That makes us think about how carefully we must research and consider our observations to make certain they are correct. There were to be many exciting puzzles and moments of inaccuracy as we continued to learn about the earth and all her mysteries. Learning how to discover what is really true is great fun and very hard sometimes.

## A Water Story

We celebrated our new fish with a wonderful story "The Rainbow Fish". This fish had beautiful shimmering scales, which it ends up sharing so everyone in the sea can be happy. After the story, I gave a tiny mylar circle to each child, which they then used as a component of an ocean picture. Before the child was presented the mylar, each made an earthkeeper promise: "I promise that I will always be curious about the wonderful world of water." We then decided it would be great fun to learn more about one of the most

My Favorite use of water is is drinking it on hot sumerdays.

amazing elements of our planet: water! We were about to embark on an adventure that would be filled with great stories and experiments and endless opportunities for observing and learning.

- We "dove" into great books. We read fact books about water and fun stories about water.

- We saw great videos about water that helped us understand the properties of water and the different states of water.

- We conducted water experiments and created some of our own experiments.

- We tried to imagine life without water and thought it would be very hard. In fact, we learned there would be no life on earth without water!

- We had a guest visit from the water department who helped us understand the importance of keeping our water clean.

- We started recycling pop cans for a secret water project. I told the children we needed 100 cans to help do something important for a creature of the earth's waters. We started charting by tens on a graph. When we had accomplished the goal of 1000 we would learn what the secret project was. (Later the children learned we were protecting a great whale, the largest creature ever to live on the earth or swim in its waters!)

## Did You Know?
## WATER FACTS

- 75% of the Earth's surface is covered with water.

- The water on earth at the time of the dinosaurs is the same water on earth today.

- About 70% of a child's body is water.

- Hailstones are one form of solid water and have been known to be as large as tennis balls!

- The farthest water falls anywhere on Earth is at Angel Falls in South America where it falls over 3200 feet!

- Rain forms when little drops of water join together and get heavy enough to fall.

- The Pacific Ocean is bigger than all the land of the Earth combined!

- If all the water on earth could fit in a gallon jug, and if you poured out the portion that was non-drinkable (too salty, polluted, or hard to get), you'd end up with one single drop.

- A running faucet puts three to five gallons of water down the drain every minute.

- We wrote a class poem about water.

- We wrote about "My Favorite Thing To Do with Water" and posted our stories at the water center.

My favrt thing to do wath wotr is swam

- Another guest came in with a huge globe of the planet and helped us understand why the earth is called the water planet. It is 3/4 water! She also helped us understand that our bodies are mostly composed of water. Water is so important. When we are thirsty, she said, that is our body calling out for its favorite drink—the drink of life—wonderful water.

- We created a water center where we had books and information to help us wonder about water.

- We recognized that water is home to many of the earth's creatures and it is important for all of us to keep it safe and clean.

- We promised always to be curious about water and remember to appreciate it more!

- At the end of our study we watched a beautiful video, *Water: The Gift of Life*, and we drank cool refreshing glasses of—you guessed it—water!

Name Sherman           Date Oct 16

**WATER EXPERIMENTS**

PREDICTIONS

I predict:
the Grape will Flot
the Laco will sink
The Coarch will sink

PROCEDURES

I did this:
AD waTher AND oil iN to jars swRom
AND waTher. Drop Grap AND
CoaRth aNoLaGo

RESULTS

I found out:
The coRcs Flots the Laco
sincs

# Books about Water

**Ardley, Neil.** *The Science Book of Water.* Harcourt Brace Jovanovich, New York, 1991.

**Ayres, Pam.** *When Dad Fills In the Garden Pond.* Alfred A. Knopf, New York, 1988.

**Chase, Edith Newlin,** and **Ron Broda.** *Waters.* North Winds, Ontario, 1993.

**Cole, Joanna.** *The Magic School Bus at the Waterworks.* Scholastic, New York, 1986.

**Dorros, Arthur.** *Follow the Water from Brook to Ocean.* HarperCollins, New York, 1991.

**Guthrie, Donna W.** *Nobiah's Well: A Modern African Folktale.* Ideals Children's Books, Nashville, Tennessee, 1993.

**Knapp, Brian.** *Science in Our World: Water.* Grolier, Danbury, Connecticut, 1991.

**Koch, Michelle.** *World Water Watch.* Greenwillow, New York, 1993.

**Mayer, Marianna.** *The Unicorn and the Lake.* Dial, New York, 1982.

**Numes, Susan.** *Tiddalick, the Frog.* Antheneum, New York, 1989.

**Peters, Lisa Westberg.** *Water's Way.* Arcade, New York, 1991.

**Pfister, Marcus.** *The Rainbow Fish.* North-South, New York, 1992.

**Rauzon, Mark J.,** and **Cynthia Overbeck Bix.** *Water, Water Everywhere.* Sierra Club, San Francisco, 1994.

**Richardson, Joy.** *The Water Cycle.* Franklin Watts, New York, 1992.

**Schmid, Eleonore.** *The Water's Journey.* North-South, New York, 1989.

**Thaler, Mike.** *In the Middle of the Puddle.* Harper and Row, New York, 1988.

## AUDIOVISUAL MATERIALS

*Down the Drain* (VHS). A Children's Television Workshop Presentation, Box HV, One Lincoln Plaza, New York, NY 10023.

*Journey of the Blob* (VHS). Bullfrog Films, P.O. Box 149, Oley, Pennsylvania 19547.

*Me and My World* (VHS). National Geographic Society, Educational Services, Washington, D.C. 20036.

*The Murky Water Caper* (VHS). The Video Project: Films and Videos for a Safe and Sustainable World, 5332 College Avenue, Suite 1E, Oakland, California, 94618.

*Water: Gift of Life* (VHS). A Nature Company Video Library Presentation, Ocean Images Production, The Nature Company, Berkeley, California.

*Water: We Can't Live Without It.* (VHS). An Educational Slide/Tape Presentation. National Wildlife Federation. National Wildlife Federation, 1412 Sixteenth Street, NW, Washington, D.C. 20036.

## REFERENCES

**Kalman, Bobbie,** and **Janine Schaub.** *Wonderful Water.* Crabtree, New York, 1992.

**Seed, Deborah.** *Water Science.* Wesley, New York, 1992.

**Stille, Darlene.** *Water Pollution.* Children's Press, Chicago, 1990.

**Taylor, Kim.** *Water.* John Wiley and Sons, New York, 1992.

**Wheeler, Jill.** *The Water We Drink.* Abdo and Daughters, Edina, Minnesota, 1990.

# For the Love of Bears

*"Great Brown Bear is walking with us,*
*salmon swimming upstream with us,*
*as we stroll a city street."* —Gary Snyder

As we investigated and celebrated the wondrous tiny monarch, we learned that it might not survive if we don't work to protect its homes. Just like us, it needs clean water and clean air. Now we were about to embark on yet another adventure with a new animal of the month—the amazing bear! We were anxious to explore the realms of this wonderful creature that has captivated us, both in the world of our imaginations and in reality since time remembered. We were to learn there are eight species of bears on the planet and we were curious about each one. Our search for "bear facts" was on. From butterflies to bears! What a marvelous world!

## Earth Minute:
### The Bear That Heard Crying

Returning to the classroom from an afternoon recess the children were delighted to notice large paw prints I had placed leading into their classroom and to the story stump. "Earth Minute!" I called, and the children moved to the carpet to await the announcement of the new *Animal of the Month*! "These could certainly not be monarch tracks," laughed Helen, and the children began to speculate what sort of creature might have such large padded footprints. As they wondered, they observed an animal track chart placed nearby. At last I unveiled a large poster that was placed on the easel, revealing the stunning scene of a mother grizzly and her two cubs. Then I shared a new book, *The Bear That Heard Crying* by Natalie Kinsey-Warnock (Cobblehill, 1993). This fascinating story, based on a true incident, tells of a little three-year-old girl lost in the woods in 1783. A black bear hears her cries and sleeps near to her during three long cold nights, saving her life before she is finally found by her frantic family. "The big black dog" the little girl told them about was in reality a bear. As we talked about this, it gave us all "paws" to think that perhaps there was a lot to learn about bears. They are of course wild animals and should not be bothered by people, but we were really curious about sorting out bear facts and fiction as we began our bear study.

# Literature Connections

The golden memory of our monarch time was strong with us as we returned to the story stump to share yet another bear tale. *The Butterfly Night of Old Brown Bear* by Nicolas van Pallandt (Farrar, Straus and Giroux, 1990) tells of a bear that collects butterflies and moths. As he pursues one particularly lovely moth to the ends of the earth, he comes to realize that perhaps its special beauty is only possible because it is flying free. We discussed what bear had learned from his adventure. "Live and let live" is something we Earthkeepers think is pretty nice! We illustrated our own imaginary bear journey. Each drew a picture of Old Brown Bear chasing the moth somewhere special on the planet. We wrote bear's thoughts on our picture and then put them all together in a class book. As we shared our writing, each child indicated where on the globe

## *Did You Know?* BEAR FACTS

○ There are eight different kinds, or *species*, of bears in the world.

○ Bears are one of the smallest mammals at birth, weighing less than 18 ounces. Many are about the size of a newborn kitten.

○ At 1,500 pounds, a grown polar bear weighs three times as much as a lion.

○ Sun bears are the smallest species of bears in the world. They weigh 60 to 100 pounds, and are only about three feet long.

○ The giant panda is the most endangered bear. Fewer than 1,000 survive. Until recently it was thought to be more closely related to the raccoon family. Biological facts now place it in the bear family.

○ Grizzly bears are the largest living omnivores and once were the most widespread of all mammals, but today they are endangered.

○ Spectacled bears get their name from the light colors around their eyes that resemble eyeglasses. They are the only bears from South America.

○ Bears communicate with huffs and blowing noises and roars.

○ The female bear is called a sow, and the male bear is called a boar.

○ Hibernation takes on many forms. Most species of bears do not hibernate. The black bear does exhibit behaviors most like what is commonly thought of as "hibernation."

○ Bears live in all climates of the world, from the freezing Arctic to the rainforest.

○ The American black bears are the most common in North America. Still, there are only 500,000 remaining.

his or her page had taken place.

We also loved another "bear books" experience. We all remembered hearing the story of "Goldilocks and the Three Bears" many times since we were little. We collected and compared different versions of the story. Then we cast our vote for our favorite version. We had different categories. The version retold by Jan Brett was chosen the "most beautiful" and *Somebody and the Three Blairs* by Marilyn Tolhurst (Orchard Books, 1990) was the "funniest." The children each wrote and illustrated a version of the famous old story. It was fun.

# Integrating the Idea:

## LANGUAGE ARTS:
## Letters to the Great Bear

Helen shared with the children a calendar filled with beautiful drawings of bears. She explained that this calendar was put together by people in Montana who really loved bears and wanted to help protect them. They were bear "experts." The children decided to write to these experts and ask them questions about what kind of bears lived there and whether they were endangered. Also, the children wondered if there was anything they needed to know that might help make sure there would always be bears. Life without them would be unbearable! A "Great Bear" bulletin board was begun where a reply would be displayed. This would become *Bear Central*, where new facts and pieces of information would be placed to be shared.

## LANGUAGE ARTS:
## Poetry: A Bear Break

We celebrated our growing bear curiosity with a poetry break. The teacher read the great poems in *Bear Hugs* by Kathleen Hague (Henry Holt, 1989). Each child then was presented with a bookmark with a bear sticker placed over a heart sticker. Perhaps they would decide to keep a place in their hearts for bears all their lives as they continued to learn more about them and their niche in our world.

## SCIENCE/MATH:
## Bear Research

We were deep into our bear books by now. We divided into eight groups to work on bear reports. We were looking for the attributes of all eight kinds of bears. One of our favorite bear fact books was *Bears* by Gallimard

decided to make a map and locate the spot were the bears we were studying lived. We already knew a lot about the map and continents because every time we read a story, we marked the place on the planet where it took place. Since we read or listened to so many stories, there were lots of chances to locate places on the map. When we shared our reports, we made a chart comparing the attributes of bears. We created bear face masks on cardboard and wrote facts on the back.

Jeunesse (Scholastic Books, 1989). We wanted to learn about bear habits and habitats. We were curious about such things as diet and size and enemies. We knew that alert Earthkeepers always need to know the facts to be good caretakers of the planet and its creatures! Parents often came to share their bear knowledge with us, or sometimes they read us their favorite bear story. It seemed they liked bears and butterflies and books as much as we did!

## SOCIAL STUDIES:
## Where in the World

One day we read *Lost!* by David McPhail, (Little Brown, 1990). A boy helps a lost bear locate where in the world is his home. We

# Celebration:
## Teddy Bear Picnic

We had worked hard. Now it was time to celebrate, so we prepared for a Teddy Bear Picnic. Each student brought a favorite personal bear as a guest and a favorite bear fact to share. We ate bear cookies and bear-shaped Jell-o and had a great time. We created venn-diagrams with a partner at the picnic as we compared the characteristics of our bears. Observation of attributes is a critical earthkeeper skill, as children learn to share thinking. We read *Jenny's Bear* by Michael Ratnett (Putnam, 1990) and enjoyed this great tale of a special bear that Jenny invited to tea. Real or not? You be your own judge!

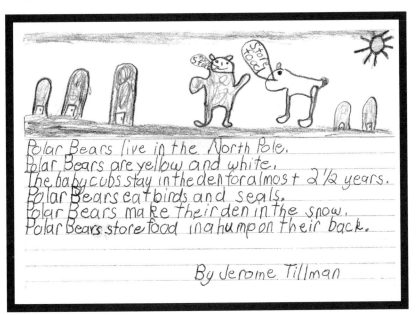

Polar Bears live in the North Pole.
Polar Bears are yellow and white,
The baby cubs stay in the den for almost 2½ years.
Polar Bears eat birds and seals.
Polar Bears make their den in the snow,
Polar Bears store food in a hump on their back.

By Jerome Tillman

need to have bears in the world. We decided to have a *Wall of Honor* for Earthkeepers like Lynn Rogers and Gary Alt who are wildlife biologists working to understand bears. We read *Two Orphan Cubs* by Barbara Brenner and May Garelick (Walker, 1989) in which Gary Alt saves two little bear cubs. One child noted that it was great that Mr. Alt could help save the baby bears just like the black bear had helped save the little girl so long ago in *The Bear that Heard Crying.*

# World Wondering:
## Honoring Earthkeepers

We were now wild about bears. One of the books we read, *Where Are My Bears?* by Ron Hirschi (Bantam, 1992), said, "Grizzlies are swift as wild horses. Grizzlies are strong. But the great grizzlies are disappearing." We didn't like that part, but we did like the next sentence: "Only you can save them." We knew we wanted to learn all we could about bears so we could help other people understand how great they are and that we will always

# Family Tie:
## Sharing Bear Tales; Bumper Stickers

We decided to celebrate what we had learned with our families. We invited them to come and share a favorite bear tale with us. We watched the wonderful animated version of *Corduroy* together and we made bear bumper stickers to place in the windows of our cars to tell the world how much we cared about the fascinating bears of our planet. As Earthkeepers we knew that part of our job forever would be to be curious and caring about our earth's bears!

Bears are a part of the Earth.

# Books about Bears

**Alexander, Sally Hobart.** *Maggie's Whopper.* MacMillan Publishing Company, New York, 1992.

**Arnosky, Jim.** *Every Autumn Comes: The Bear.* G .P. Putman's Sons, New York, 1992.

**Betz, Dieter.** *The Bear Family.* Tambourine Books, Morrow, New York, 1991.

**Bird, E. J.** *How Do Bears Sleep?* Carolrhoda Books, Minneapolis, 1990.

**Brenner, Barbara,** and **May Garelick.** *Two Orphan Cubs.* Walker, New York, 1989.

**Brett, Jan.** *Berlioz the Bear.* Scholastic, New York, 1991.

**Brett, Jan.** *Goldilocks and the Three Bears.* Dodd, Mead and Company, New York, 1987.

**Carlstrom, Nancy White.** *It's About Time, Jesse Bear.* MacMillan, New York, 1990.

**Fair, Jeff.** *Bears for Kids.* North Word Press, Minacqua, Wisconsin, 1991.

**Falk, Barbara Bustetter.** *Grusha.* Harper-Collins, New York, 1993.

**Greenaway, Theresa.** *Amazing Bears.* Alfred A. Knopf, New York, 1992.

**Gill, Shelley.** *Alaska's Three Bears.* Paws IV Publishing, Homer, Alaska, 1990.

**Hague, Kathleen.** *Alphabears, ABC Book.* Scholastic, New York, 1984.

**Hague, Kathleen.** *Bear Hugs.* Henry Holt, New York, 1989.

**Hirschi, Ron.** *Where Are My Bears?* Bantam Books, New York, 1992.

**Jeunesse, Gallimard,** and **Laura Bour.** *Bears.* Scholastic, New York, 1989.

**Kinsey-Warnock, Natalie,** and **Helen Kinsey.** *The Bear That Heard Crying.* Cobblehill, New York, 1993.

**Krause, Ute.** *Nora and the Great Bear.* Dial, New York, 1989.

**Kuchalla, Susan.** *Now I Know Bears.* Troll, New Yoirk, 1982.

**Lind, Alan.** *Black Bear Cub.* Sound Prints, Norwalk, Connecticut, 1994.

**McPhail, David.** *Lost!* Little, Brown, Boston, 1990.

**Newman, Nannette.** *There's a Bear in the Bath.* Harcourt Brace, San Diego, 1994.

**Ratnett, Michael.** *Jenny's Bear.* G. P. Putman, New York, 1991.

**Ryder, Joanne.** *White Bear, Ice Bear.* Morrow Junior Books, New York, 1989.

**Schoenherr, John.** *Bear.* Scholastic, New York, 1991(RJA45406-4).

**Stirling, Ian.** *Bears.* Sierra Club Books for Children, San Francisco, 1992.

**Tejima, Keizaburo.** *The Bear's Autumn.* Green Tiger Press, La Jolla, California, 1986.

**Tolhurst, Marilyn.** *Somebody and the Three Blairs.* Orchard Books, New York, 1990.

**Waddell, Martin.** *Let's Go Home, Little Bear.* Candlewick Press, Cambridge, Massachusetts, 1991.

**Wallace, Karen.** *Bears in the Forest.* Candlewick Press, Cambridge, Massachusetts, 1994.

## VIDEOS

*Corduroy and Other Bear Stories.* A Children's Circle (VHS), Weston Woods, Weston, Connecticut 06883-1199, 1986.

*The Biggest Bears* (VHS). SkyRiver Films, 3700 Woodland Drive, Suite 100, Anchorage, Alaska 99517.

# For the Love of Bats

*"All the bright day, as the mother sleeps,
She folds her wings about the sleeping child."*

—Randall Jarrell

It is October—prime "bat fever" time! So . . . what better choice could there be for our Animal of the Month? What a golden opportunity to explore the murky mythology that surrounds our often bad bat-attitudes in an effort to do what good education can do best—shed light on the truth! With great anticipation, we initiated yet a new journey into the wildly intriguing world of bats. We had followed the migration of magnificent butterflies and explored the wonder of bears. Would the patterns we might discover in our study of bats show any similarities to the lives of these animals, we wondered? We were curious Earthkeepers, so we tuned up all our senses and were ready to begin.

## Earth Minute:
### Going "Batty"

One afternoon in early October as Helen and the children returned from lunch, I met them outside their classroom door. When they entered the room, I asked them to main-

tain a total Earthkeeper Silence. On their desks were paper and pencils. They were to observe silently. They immediately saw the large colony of paper bats that now inhabited the front board. Soft "Oohs!" and a few "Yuks!" could be heard. As they sat down, I invited them to spend five minutes to write

down "What I know about Bats." When they had completed their task, each child was to turn the paper over and work on a bat illustration or scene until all students were done. With the "silence" still in effect, I placed a "Bat-Marker" on each child's desk. This was an inch-square piece of paper bearing the image of a bat on front. The children were asked to turn to the blank side. They were to respond to the choice of two statements: Bats make me feel happy, or, Bats make me feel sad. They were to draw a happy face or a sad face on the paper to indicate their response. When all this was done, we talked.

Working together, we listed all our different feelings about bats. The markers were then used to create a graph of the *Bat Attitude* of the class. Misconceptions were running rampant! I then announced that the bat was the new Animal of the Month. "But it's not an animal; it's a bird!" said Jacob. "Why don't we check that out, along with your other bat ideas," I said. I was met with enthusiastic responses. To celebrate the beginning of a new Earthkeeper study, I read *Bat Time* by Ruth Horowitz (Four Winds Press, 1991). By the end of this story about a little girl who loves to watch bats with her father, the children began to think that they might want to be "Bat-watchers" in addition to their other Earthkeeper duties!

# Literature Connections:

## Teaching with Books About Bats

We were all really excited about our new Animal of the Month.

- We took a vote on the question "Is a bat a bird?"

- We listened to a great story called *Stellaluna* by Janell Cannon (HBJ, 1993). We loved this tale of a bat that is

## *Did You Know?* BAT FACTS

- Bats are the only flying mammals. Almost 1/4 of the world's mammal species are bats.

- Bats are not blind. Most use sonar and echolocation to locate food and to survive. Fruit bats, however, have well-developed senses of sight and smell.

- Bats are amazing acrobats and can swoop, soar, twist, turn, and dip with their quiet, graceful movements.

- Bats are good parents. Baby bats are called pups.

- Bats are found on every continent except Antarctica.

- The bat has a small thumb with a useful claw on the edge of its wing.

- Bats are clean animals. They hang upside down and can lick their wings clean and groom their faces using their thumbs.

- Bats waste droppings are called *guano* and are useful fertilizer.

- Some bats eat up to 600 mosquitoes an hour; other bats eat frogs, fish, and even fruit.

- The bones in the bat wings are like the finger bones in our hands. The scientific name for bats is *Chiroptera*, which means "hand-wing."

- Bat homes include caves, tall trees, bushes, and barns.

- Bats are invaluable pollinators and pest controllers.

- Bats come in many sizes. The smallest weighs less than a penny. The largest, with a 6-foot wing span, weighs about two pounds.

- Bats are often threatened because of loss of habitat, toxics in the air and water, and human ignorance.

separated from its mother and tries to live with birds.

- We listed all the ways that the bat in the story was not like a bird. It was interesting to read the great bat facts at the end of this book, too.

- Each time we learned a new bat fact, we wrote it on white paper and attached it to one of the black paper bats that had been removed from the front board. We soon had real bat facts flying all over the walls of the room. We also decided a bat is definitely not a bird.

Someone is always losing a tooth in first grade, and one day Sarah lost one of hers. It seemed the perfect time to share *Loose Tooth* by Steven Kroll (Scholastic, 1984). This tale of twin bats, Fangs and Flapper, is pure fun.

After enjoying it together we discussed which facts about bats mentioned in the story might actually be true "bat facts" in real life. It can be great fun being a "Fact or Fiction Truth Detective"!

- We liked the names the author had chosen for the bats and discussed other ones that might have been used to suggest different bat characteristics. We thought of names like Midnight and Crooked Wing.

- We each drew and named our own personal bat mascot to be our bat buddy throughout this bat information search time.

- We learned that we were to be assisted in our library research by fourth grade partners. We would have a twin just like Fangs and Flapper.

# Integrating the Idea:

## LANGUAGE ARTS: Bat Buddies Begin

We met our Bat Buddies in the classroom one day. We shared with them some of the facts we had already learned about bats. Then we went to the library to research. We were supposed to find five Bat Facts. With our buddies we searched in books and on computers. We were going to use the information to write a fiction story based on true facts about bats. This collaboration proved to be a wonderful cooperative learning venture for all involved. We met several times with our Bat Buddies to work on our story. When we were done writing, we went to their classroom to type it on their computers.

## LANGUAGE ARTS: Poetry Break—The Bat Poet

One day we read the beautiful story poem "A Bat is Born" from *The Bat Poet* by Randell Jarrell (Doubleday, 1964). We loved this story of a mother bat flying with her baby clinging close. It made us want to write poems about holding on tight during such a magical trip, so we did just that! Bat poems flew from our pens.

## SCIENCE/MATH: Bat Survey

By now we were bats about bats! We returned to our old chart to see if some of us had changed our minds about them. Boy, had we! We were curious how others felt about bats, so together we created a Bat Survey. We made up ten true-or-false questions like "Bats are blind, T/F." Children took the survey home for parents to answer and we also asked others at school. We learned that not everyone knew as much about bats as we did. "My mom just hates them!" said Sarah. "She doesn't understand yet." The survey was fun.

## SOCIAL STUDIES:
## Bat Map

I read a wonderful African story, *A Promise to the Sun* by Tololwa Mollel (Little, Brown, 1992). This porquoi tale explains why bats fly only at night. It made us think how bats are in stories from many lands; and in fact, live on every continent except Antarctica. We made a "Bat Map of the World" and included this on our "Bats Are Beautiful" bulletin board display, along with our Bat Buddy stories and art. Children were allowed to use any materials they wished to construct an original bat design. These hung above the board.

## Celebrations:
### Bat Man Visits

- We invited our Bat Buddies to come hear a wonderful expert speaker who loved bats as much as we did. We gave him our Earthkeeper award for his work with bats. We served a fruit salad treat we had made. We used fruits like the banana that depend on the bat for pollination.

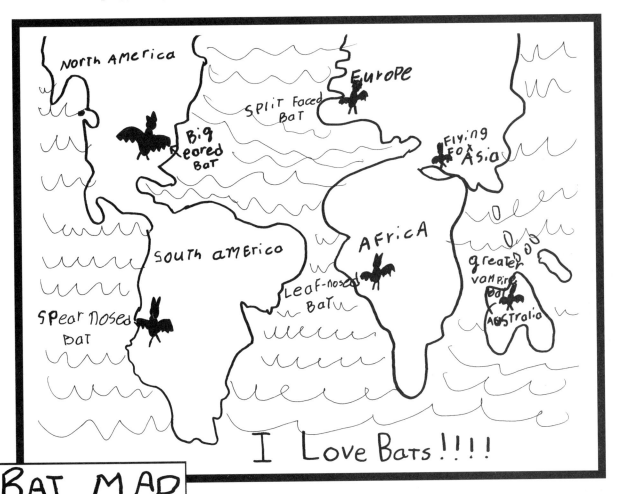

BAT MAP

# World Wondering:

## Sharing Our "Bat" Attitude

We wanted to share our bat awareness, so we wrote a class letter and sent it to the "Letters to the Editor" of our town newspaper. "Be nice to bats," we urged. "Learn the facts! A bat eats thousands of insects. If the bats eat them, then these pests don't have to be killed with insect sprays that can contain chemicals that can be dangerous for us all".

We learned a lot more; but most importantly, we learned that bats are nothing to be frightened of. If you don't pick up a sick bat, then a bat can never hurt you. Bats are marvelous creatures and should be protected, not feared. As we were talking, Jenna made a great observation: "Bats hibernate like bears and migrate like butterflies." The circles of nature are fascinating!

## Family Tie:

## A Night at the Bat House

Barbara Bash tells us in her excellent book, *Shadows of the Night* (Sierra Club Books for Children, 1993), that "in China, the bat is a symbol of good fortune and wisdom and is often painted in red—the color of joy." We decided to do one more thing for bats. We designed red-colored bat invitations to send to our parents to invite them to attend a Bat House Night. We wanted to build bat houses to place in the trees around school or other good sites. We had donated lumber and several carpenter parents so we were set. All the children were involved in the dedication of these structures. They were exhilarated to be making a difference in their world. Bat houses need to be placed ten to fifteen feet from the ground in a tree or on a structure. Bash also says the house needs to face the morning sun. It should be open at the bottom, with vertical slats inside that are 1/4" to 1" apart. They are made from rough, unpainted wood, so the bats can get a foothold. Plans are available from numerous sources, such as Bat Conservation International.

Bats Hag upsidown
Wan tay Seelp
Bats Halp us
Bats com awt at
Nart

Bats Are Hammless.

Bats ar Good.

We love bats.

Bats are Beautefl.

Will protakt bats!

Bats Are helppull t Othenvirement!

# Books about Bats

**Bash, Barbara**. *Shadows of Night*. Sierra Club Books, San Francisco, 1993.

**Bruchac, Joseph**. *The Great Ball Game: A Muskogee Story*. Dial, New York, 1994.

**Cannon, Janell**. *Stellaluna*. Harcourt Brace, New York, 1993.

**Clark, Emma Chichester**. *Lunch with Aunt Augusta*. Dial Books for Young Readers, New York, 1991.

**Freeman, Don**. *Hattie the Backstage Bat*. Viking Press, New York, 1970.

**Green, Carl R.,** and **William R. Sanford**. *The Little Brown Bat*. Crestwood House, Mankato, Minnesota, 1986.

**Greenaway, Frank**. *Amazing Bats*. Alfred A. Knopf, New York, 1991.

**Horowitz, Ruth**. *Bat Time*. Four Winds Press, New York, 1991.

**Ivy, Bill**. *Bats: Nature's Children*. Grolier, Danbury, Connecticut, 1986.

**Jarrell, Randall**. *A Bat is Born*. Doubleday, Garden City, New York, 1978.

**Kroll, Steven**. *Loose Tooth*. Scholastic, New York, 1984.

**Lovett, Sarah**. *Extremely Weird Bats*. John Muir Publications, Santa Fe, New Mexico, 1991.

**Maestro, Betsy,** and **Giulio Maestro.** *Bats, Night Fliers*. Scholastic, New York, 1994.

**Milton, Joy**. *Bats: Creatures of the Night*. Putnam, New York, 1993.

**Mollel, Tololwa M**. *A Promise to the Sun*. Little, Brown, Boston, 1992.

**Pringle, Laurence**. *Batman*. Charles Scribner's Sons, New York, 1991.

**Schlein, Miriam**. *Billions of Bats*. J. P. Lippincott, New York, 1982.

**Selsam, Millicent,** and **Joyce Hunt**. *A First Look at Bats*. Walker and Co., New York, 1991.

**Stuart, Dee**. *Bats, Mysterious Flyers of the Night*. Carolrhoda, Minneapolis, 1994.

**Ungerer, Tomi**. *Rufus*. Dell Publishing, New York, 1961.

**Voight, Virginia Frances**. *Little Brown Bat*. G. P. Putnam's Sons, New York, 1969.

*Zoobooks. Bats*. Wildlife Education, San Diego, 1989.

## VIDEO

*Very Elementary Bats* (VHS). Bat Conservation International, P.O. Box 162603, Austin, Texas 78716.

Bat

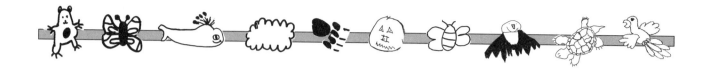

# Native Americans

*"We are part of the earth and it is part of us.*
*The earth does not belong to us. We belong to the earth."*

—Chief Seattle

We were learning much about the earth. Now autumn and its time of harvest gave us a strong need to honor the ancient memory our land held for her first Earthkeepers—the Native Americans. "The People," as they often called themselves, referred to the land on which they lived as Turtle Island. It had been their home for more than 10,000 years before being "discovered" by Columbus. In all that time The People had existed in harmony with Mother Earth and her creatures. The waters and the air remained pure and the bounty of the land was endless. It seems sad to us that Native Americans along with their cherished buffalo, eagles, and wolves were to be threatened with extinction in the years that would follow. The events that unfolded after 104 colonists made their home at Jamestown shaped all our lives. Turtle Island's destiny was forever altered. With respect for their heritage, we begin our study of the first Earthkeepers of Turtle Island. We honor

them and know their wisdom has much to teach all the earth's children.

## Earth Minute:
### An Ancient Campfire

When Helen and the children returned from recess they knew something was up! A small tub of earth had been placed next to the story stump and a hand shovel was stuck in the soil. I came from the back room and called "Earth Minute." We sat down, then I shared a lovely book, *Under the Moon* by Dyan Sheldon (Dial, 1994). In the story a little girl named Jenny finds an arrowhead while digging in her backyard. She is enchanted by it and tries to imagine what the world might have been like long ago. She camps out with the arrowhead in her hand. A dream takes her on a magical journey back to a time when "the land was as open as the sky." She meets the real owner of the arrowhead and sits in the circle by his campfire. She loves this time long ago, "when everything on earth had a voice and a heart, and time was measured by the changing of the moon." Everyone loved the story, especially when Jenny decided to return the arrowhead to the earth. "It's like she wanted to give it back to her friend," said Sarah. The children had almost forgotten about the tub of dirt. Then I placed my hand on the shovel. "Let's see what we have here,"

I said and gently uncovered (to no one's surprise) an arrowhead! There was much excitement as the children learned that their next unit of study was to be Native Americans, "the first Earthkeepers"! "There is much more to Native peoples than arrows!" said Helen.

# Literature Connections

## Teaching with Books About The People

The morning of the second day of our study we were surprised to find a huge tepee where the story stump used to be! "We have much to learn before we enter our tepee," said Helen.

- **Tepee rules.** We gathered in a circle in front of the wondrous tepee and discussed guidelines! We would enter it with quiet Earthkeeper voices of great respect as a place for reading or telling stories. Our tepee faced east to greet Father Sun.

- **Importance of the circle.** We read a story, *Ceremony in the Circle of Life* by White Deer of Autumn (Beyond Words Publishing, 1991). We were to listen for references to circles as we enjoyed the story. There were many!

- **A circle chart.** We made a big circle on the board and recorded the different references to circles. We decided to add to this all during our study of The People.

- **Calculating ages.** The story told us there are four seasons in the complete circle of the year. The boy in the story had lived nine complete circles so he was nine years old. We loved thinking of our own age in this way of the circle!

- **Selecting a native name.** We liked Little Turtle's name. We decided to choose a personal name for use during our study. We wanted our name to have something

## Did You Know? NATIVE AMERICAN FACTS

- ○ Native Americans had been on this continent for more than 10,000 years before Christopher Columbus "discovered" them.

- ○ Native Americans refer to themselves and their tribes not as Indians, but as The People.

- ○ The first hi-rise apartment complexes in this country were built by the Anasazi Indians thousands of years ago.

- ○ Native Americans domesticated over forty plants, including the white potato, corn, peanuts, and tomatoes.

- ○ The turkey was domesticated by Southwest Indians. They held "Brother Turkey" in great respect.

- ○ Native Americans developed the snowshoe, sun-goggles, and the kayak.

- ○ Navajo language is so complex that during World War II, they were asked by the U.S. government to develop a secret code based on their language. It was never broken by the enemy.

- ○ Woven robes were created by the Pueblo Indians long before they acquired looms from the Spanish.

- ○ The salmon was as important to the Northwest Indians as the buffalo was to the Plains Indians.

- ○ Half of our states in the U.S. and numerous cities derive their names from Native American origins.

- ○ In 1924 all Native Americans were made citizens of the United States.

- ○ In 1968 The People were given the right to govern themselves on their reservations.

to do with our feelings for the earth. We had learned that names were special to The People so we made our choice carefully. When we were done Dillon said we should have chosen our Native American name and not Indian name. We talked about that!

- **A video about listening!** We were becoming sensitive to looking for circles and were now ready to test our Earthkeeper ears as we watched a video of a wonderful story by Byrd Baylor and Peter Parnall called *The Other Way to Listen* (Scribners, 1978). The People were great listeners, and we were working on it!

# Integrating the Idea:

## LANGUAGE ARTS: Tales of Tricksters

We learned that many tales of The People have a character who is a trickster. Sometimes he is good and sometimes not. Coyote and Raven are two such characters. We read tales such as *Raven* by Gerald McDermott (Harcourt Brace, 1993) and *Coyote Steals the Blanket* retold by Janet Stevens (Holiday House, 1993). We kept a chart of each tale we read during "Tale Time." We wrote down who the trickster was, what he wanted, how he tried to get it, whether he was successful, what tribe the tale was from, and finally we listed the characteristics of the "trickster". We really liked these characters!

## LANGUAGE ARTS: Tying Knots on a Counting Rope/Oral Storytelling

One day the school principal came to visit. Together with Helen he read *Knots on a Counting Rope* by Bill Martin and John Archambault (Henry Holt, 1987). The children loved this beautiful tale of a blind boy and his elderly grandfather who is teaching him a special story. "Tell me the story again, Grandfather. Tell me who I am," it begins. Each time the story has been told, another knot is tied in a "counting rope"—a way of marking the passage of time. Soon the boy, through repetition, will be able to tell the story on his own!

- **A discussion of oral traditions.** I shared with the children that Native Americans did not have a written language for centuries and so the storyteller was important for passing on tales and traditions by word of mouth.

- **Pictographs and petroglyphs.** Some events were recorded using drawn symbols. We learned some of these and tried to record imagined events. We observed pictures of symbols on cave walls from long ago.

- **Our own oral story.** We decided to create oral stories of our own lives and practice telling them in an interesting way. We sent notes home to parents, asking them to help us. Each child was given an 18-inch piece of rope that was to be their personal "counting rope" to use as they learned their story. These stories would be recorded in a few weeks to keep forever, although by then they would be stored in our memory! One child wanted a second rope to record each new story she read or heard.

- **An oral storyteller.** To help us appreciate oral stories we gathered in a circle by the tepee, turned off the lights, and listened to a tape of *The Boy Who Lived with the Bears* by the wonderful Native American storyteller Joseph Bruchac. It felt like he was there with us as we were practicing the art of listening!

## LANGUAGE ARTS: Poetry of a Peaceful People

SNOW moon January

We loved the gentleness of the boy Hiawatha in a version of the poem illustrated by Susan Jeffers (Dial, 1983). We did not understand all the words, but we were swept away by the feelings. We drew a group mural of the poem, each adding our favorite part. Longfellow, the poet, lived long ago and really respected The People.

SNOW MOON    HUNGER MOON    CROW MOON    GRASS MOON    PLANTING MOON

HEAT MOON    THUNDER MOON    HUNTING MOON    FALLING LEAF MOON    BEAVER MOON

Falling LEAF moon

October

## SCIENCE/MATH: Thirteen Moons on Turtle's Back

We read another beautiful series of story poems, *Thirteen Moons on Turtle's Back: A Native American Year of Moons* by Joseph Bruchac and Jonathan London (Philomel, 1992). The native people had strong connections with the natural world. They observed carefully the changing of the moon and the seasons. I shared drawings that had been given to me years ago by an elderly artist. They represented the seasons of the Sioux moon, which correspond roughly to traditional calendar months. He had found them in *Indian Sign Language* by William Tomkins. We drew the one that would most closely relate to our own birthday month, but we loved them all and their connections with the earth.

## SOCIAL STUDIES: Turtle Island Adventure/ Diving into the Facts

We read a totally terrific book, *Turtle Island ABC: A Gathering of Native American Symbols* by Gerald Hausman (Harper Collins, 1994). We wanted to learn all we could about The People and this book was a great help! Each letter taught us something special.

- **Creating a "Turtle Island Alphabet" board.** Each of us took one letter to illustrate. We crinkled brown sack paper to give our drawings an authentic look!

- **Sending feather messages.** Our favorite symbol was "F" for Feather! Feather travels on the wind and can carry a special wish to places like the Rainbow or the Sun. We drew a feather, wrote our wish, and addressed it to our chosen destination.

- **Feather and bead necklaces.** We made necklaces of beads in a pattern and pressed our own "Wish Feather" into the center bead. The People loved the "roundness" of beads. They made them from seeds, minerals, and parts of animals. They wore them with pride.

## SOCIAL STUDIES: "Jonathan's Wish" — The Environment Emerges

We decided to rewrite the traditional Thanksgiving play making a determined effort to remove Native American stereotypes and celebrate their wisdom. We wrote a play about Jonathan, a pilgrim boy who is helped by The People. We researched to learn about the ways of Native Americans. We enjoyed *10 Little Rabbits* by Virginia Grossman and Sylvia Long (Chronicle, 1991).

- **Visit from an expert.** A Native American woman came to visit, and shared many artifacts. We learned that our tepee was only one type of Native American home. Construction was determined by the materials available where the tribe lived. Bark, animal hides, and even snow could be used. It was important that the house be in harmony with Mother Earth. We made drawings and models of the different kinds of Native American homes.

- **Dreamcatchers.** We read the book *Dreamcatcher* by Audrey Osofsky (Orchard, 1992). We loved the tale of the Ojibway Indians who treasured good dreams and wove nets to catch bad dreams and protect their children. We then made our own dreamcatchers from willow and yarn as we listened to Native American music!

- **Pots from the earth.** We made pots from clay—another gift of Mother Earth. Native potters respected the clay, which they believed contained the ashes of their ancestors. Some of us made turtles to honor this creature that legend says holds the earth on her back.

- **Sandpainting.** From white sand colored with chalk we fashioned paintings on black cardboard. We knew that real sandpaintings were sacred and often created and destroyed in only a few hours as a part of special ceremonies. We used yellow, red, black, and white sand for the four directions or races in the Circle of Life.

- **"Native-foods" expert.** The head of the school cafeteria helped us plan an authentic Native American menu for our feast to share with our parents. Many of our best foods came to us from The People, like corn, beans, squash, and even peanuts. Turkeys were also domesticated by Native Americans, and they held them in great respect as wise creatures.

Sometimes they kept them more as pets than for food!

- **"Wisdom of the People" Center.** We created a display under the Turtle Island Alphabet Board where we could place artifacts from our families. We would touch these only with our eyes and not with our hands. One father brought in an axe head he had found in his farm field. No end to the wonders!

# Celebrations:

## What I Am Thankful For!

We had learned so much about Native American people, and we wanted to say thank you! We made cutouts of items they had given us, like corn. On these we wrote something we were thankful for. We displayed them together with other notes of thanks.

I am thankful for wolfs and trees and birds and clouds and flowers and dragonflys and bushes and Land and the wonderful great good fantastic earth.

# World Wondering:

## Saluting Turtle's Friend

I read a story, *And Still the Turtle Watched* by Sheila MacGill (Dial, 1991). It tells of a stone turtle that was carved centuries ago by a Native American to be the eyes of Manitou and watch over the people. Time passed and many things changed. He was forgotten, then treated with disrespect, and finally saved by a man with a special heart. We wrote letters of thanks to this man at the New York Botanical Gardens who had been Turtle's savior. We are glad that times of respect seem to be returning to the earth, at least in the hearts of the children!

# Family Tie:

## A Play to Honor The People

We were now ready! The lines had been learned! The research had been done! The authentic feast had been prepared! We performed well honoring the contributions of these amazing First American Earthkeepers. When all was finished we watched a wonderful video, *All Things Are Connected*, which uses the words of Chief Seattle with pictures to help us understand the Native American respect for the earth. These children are young and full of truth. The times perhaps are changing!

# Books about Native Americans

Bierhorst, John. *On the Road of the Stars: Native American Night Poems.* Macmillan, New York, 1994.

Bruchac, Joseph, and Jonathan London. *Thirteen Moons on Turtle's Back.* Philomel, New York, 1992.

Bruchac, Joseph. *Fox Song.* Philomel, New York, 1993.

Bruchac, Joseph. *The First Strawberries.* Dial, New York, 1993.

Caduta, Michael J. and Joseph Bruchac. *Keepers of the Animals: Native American Stories and Wildlife Activities for Children.* Fulcrum, Golden, Colorado, 1991.

Carlstrom, Nancy White. *Northern Lullaby.* Philomel, New York, 1992.

Cohen, Caron Lee. *The Mud Pony.* Scholastic, New York, 1988.

Cohlene, Terri. *Turquoise Boy, A Navajo Legend.* Watermill, Rahway, New Jersey, 1990.

de Paola, Tomie. *The Legend of Bluebonnet.* Putnams, New York, 1983.

de Paola, Tomie. *The Popcorn Book.* Holiday, New York, 1978.

Franklin, Kristine L. *The Shepherd Boy.* Atheneum, New York, 1994.

Goble, Paul. *The Girl Who Loved Wild Horses.* Scholastic, New York, 1993

Goble, Paul. *The Lost Children.* Bradbury, New York, 1993.

Grossman, Virginia. *Ten Little Rabbits.* Chronicle, San Francisco, 1991.

Hausman, Gerald. *Turtle Island ABC.* HarperCollins, New York, 1994.

Jeffers, Susan. *Brother Eagle, Sister Sky.* Dial, New York, 1991.

Longfellow, Henry Wadsworth. *Hiawatha.* Dial, New York, 1983.

MacGill-Callahan, Sheila. *And Still the Turtle Watched.* Dial, New York, 1991.

Martin, Bill Jr., and John Archambault. *Knots on a Counting Rope.* Henry Holt, New York, 1987.

Martin, Rafe. *The Rough-Face Girl.* Putnam's Sons, New York, 1992.

McDermott, Gerald. *Raven.* Harcourt Brace, New York, 1993.

McGovern, Ann. *If You Lived with the Sioux Indians.* Scholastic, New York, 1992.

Medearis, Angela Shelf. *Dancing with the Indians.* Holiday, New York, 1991.

Moroney, Lynn. *The Boy Who Loved Bears: A Pawnee Tale.* Children's Press, Chicago, 1994.

Nunes, Susan. *Coyote Dreams.* Antheneum, New York, 1988.

Oughton, Jerrie. *How the Stars Fell into the Sky.* Houghton Mifflin, Boston, 1992.

Rodanas, Kristina. *Dragonfly's Tale.* Clarion, New York, 1991.

Root, Phyllis. *Coyote and the Magic Words.* Lothrop, Lee and Shepard, New York. 1993.

Sheldon, Dyan. *Under the Moon.* Dial, New York, 1994.

Skofield, James. *Crow Moon, Worm Moon.* Four Winds Press, New York, 1990.

Sneve, Virginia Driving Hawk. *The Sioux: A First Americans Book.* Holiday House, New York, 1993.

Steptoe, John. *The Story of Jumping Mouse.* Lothrop, Lee and Shepard, New York, 1984.

**Stevens, Janet.** *Coyote Steals the Blanket.* Holiday House, New York, 1993.

**Taylor, C.J.** *How We Saw the World.* Tundra. Books, Plattsburgh, New York, 1993.

**Taylor, C.J.** *The Secret of the White Buffalo.* Tundra Books, Plattsburgh, New York, 1993.

**Taylor, Harriet Peck.** *Coyote Places the Stars.* Bradbury Press, New York, 1993.

**VanLaan, Nancy.** *Rainbow Crow.* Alfred A. Knopf, New York, 1989.

**Walters, Anna Lee.** *The Two-Legged Creature.* Northland, Flagstaff, Arizona, 1993.

**Yolen, Jane.** *Encounter.* Harcourt Brace Jovanovich, New York, 1992.

## AUDIOVISUAL MATERIALS

*All Things Are Connected (VHS).* North Carolina Wildlife Resources Commission Division of Conservation Education, 512 N. Salisbury Street, Raleigh, NC 27604-1188.

*Dream Catcher* (CD). Tokeya Inajin, Kevin Locke, P.O. Box 1460, Redway, CA 95560.

*The Boy Who Lived with the Bears and Other Iroquois Stories* (audio tape). HarperCollins, 10 East 53rd St., New York, NY 10022.

*The Other Way to Listen* (VHS). Best film and Video Corp., Great Neck, NY 11021.

MY INdian name is

Circle OF LiFe

Because I Love Nature

53

# For the Love of Wolves

*"Until he extends his circle of compassion*
*To all living things, man will not himself find peace."*
—Albert Schweitzer

Native Americans revered the wolf. Historically, however, few animals have been as maligned as this wondrous creature. Driven to the near brink of extinction, there are approximately 1,000 wolves surviving in the wilds of the lower forty-eight states. The wolf was to be the Animal of the Month during November and early December. Some children's literature has let this animal down, provoking deep and unwarranted fear. It seemed time to look again at the wolf through the eyes of an Earthkeeper. There is much to be learned!

## Earth Minute:
### A "Good-Dream" Wolf

The morning was new and the day overcast as I came to the classroom and softly began the earth chant. This was the signal for the children to join in and follow me to the carpet in front of the story stump. (This was the trunk of an old tree that served as a teacher's chair at these special sharing times). When gathered there, the children watched as I placed a large earth bag with great ceremony in front of them. "In this bag is one of the earth's greatest treasures. Native Americans have great respect and love for it, and so do I." After some speculating as to the bag's contents, I gently removed a large stuffed toy wolf. (One could use a picture of

a wolf as an alternative). There was a burst of reactions from "I knew it!" to one little girl who pulled back in genuine fear. "Kelly, why are you frightened of the wolf?" I asked. Typical of many children she responded, "It wants to eat me!" I suggested that a little study of wolves might be in order. We remembered other times we had misunderstood animals. "I used to be scared about bats until I learned about them. Maybe we could help you about wolves," said Bethany.

So it was! For the next few weeks Helen

and her class would explore the wolf. We would discover the source of many of our fears and sort out what was real and what was not real. I read the beautiful Native American legend *Dream Wolf* by Paul Goble (Bradbury Press, 1990). The wolf in this story saves the children—a different experience for Kelly and other victims of the "Big Bad Wolf" bias. Our wolf was placed in the fake snow (acquired from the discards of a mall display) and in front of real prairie grass as the children prepared to study the wolf that had come to their classroom.

# Integrating the Idea

## Teaching with Books About Wolves

**A History Lesson:** We read *The First Dog* by Jan Brett (HBJ, 1988), which is an imaginative adventure about the development of a friendship between a cave boy and a wolf-like creature. In reality, it is thought that people and wolves were not enemies until about 12,000 years ago when farming began. After animals began to be domesticated and raised by farmers, wolves got into trouble by taking a few of the farmer's animals. People then began killing wolves and now they are almost all gone. We wrote stories about "How I Became Friends with the World's First Wolf." It was fun wondering.

## *Did You Know?* WOLF FACTS

○ All domestic dogs are descended from wolves. Both wolf parents help supply the pups with food and train them. All adults in the pack help care for the young.

○ Wolves live in families called packs, and each pack has two leaders, the Alpha male and Alpha female.

○ Wolves can hear a watch ticking thirty feet away.

○ Adult wolves weigh from 57 pounds to more than 170 pounds, depending on where they live.

○ Wolf puppies are born helpless, with their eyes shut and weighing about a pound.

○ Wolves howl when they are happy or excited, or to establish territory, or when they want to communicate with each other and keep their packs together.

○ Wolves have been known to travel for hours at nearly twenty miles per hour.

○ It has been estimated that there are probably fewer than 2,000 wolves alive in all the United States, outside of Alaska.

○ Wolves have been misunderstood and persecuted for centuries. They have been shot, poisoned, and trapped mercilessly. Wolves have been extinct in England since 1500.

○ In the U.S. today, there are 100,000 to 300,000 wolf-dog hybrids. These are a point of controversy. Owners love them, but the U.S. Humane Society fears these animals can never be fully domesticated and unfortunate incidents will bring back images of the "Big Bad Wolf." Wolves belong in the wild.

**A Comparison of Tales:** We read two great versions of a story about a little girl and a gunnywolf. We read *The Gunnywolf* by A. Delany (Harper and Row, 1988) and *The Gunniwolf* retold by Wilhelmina Harper (E.P. Dutton, 1967). We made a class list of the ways the stories were alike and different. We liked singing the alphabet song using a silly gunnywolf voice in the version by Delaney. We imagined Kelly was the little girl in the story, and that she was not so afraid of wolves now!

**Wolf Facts, Not Fiction:** As much as we enjoyed the fun fiction stories, we really wanted some facts. One child who had been a somewhat reluctant reader pleaded, "I've got to have some more wolf books. I just love them." Our solution was to locate books like *Wild, Wild Wolves* by Joyce Milton (Random House, 1992) and Greene's *Gray Wolf* (Enslow, 1993). We made *Wolf Fact Cards* to display on the "Wonderful Wolf Bulletin Board."

## WOLF FACTS

WOLF'S EAR VARE SHie.
WOLF'S EAR NOT BiG AND BAD. WOLF'S EAR RELADi TO DOG'S. WOLF'S FUR FRR CHACH'S KULR WTP iN THE WiTR.
WOLF'S EAR iNDA HRBD

Wolf packs rarely attack humans They usually try to avoid contact with people.

Wolfs are wild

Each pups Eyes are closed wane There fist born.

"The Big Good Wolf"
By Katie

"Some paple think wolves are bad. But thay rely art. Wolves are more afrad ov you thin you are afrad ov thim. Thar are miny cins ov wolves in the world. Most male wolves wigh considerably more than 100 pounds!

# Integrating the Idea:

## LANGUAGE ARTS: "The Big Good Wolf," a Class Story

We reminisced together about the many versions of the big bad wolf tale. We even read a few. Sarah suggested it was time to write a new version, "The Big Good Wolf!" We all felt that was a terrific idea and began writing a class story together. The wolf went to grandma's house all right, but not to eat her. He came bringing home Little Red who had become lost in the woods. We made a group mural to illustrate our story.

### Wolves

Wolves, Wolves Wonderful Wolves.
They Live in the Wild They hunt in Packs.
Don't Be scard of the Wolves you See
Because their Beautiful as can Be.
Save The Wolves every Day, IT would
Be So sad iF They went away.

by Kathryn and sarah

## POETRY BREAK: Partner Poems

We paired up with partners. The beautiful sounds of Paul Winter's *Common Ground*, complete with wolf calls, was playing softly as I read the lavishly illustrated book, *The Eyes of the Gray Wolf* by Jonathan London (Chronicle Books, 1993). The book was so lovely; it was like looking at a poem. We sat quietly with our partner and together we created a Partner Poem, trying to catch in our words some of the wonder we felt for this fascinating animal. We hoped wolves would not remain forever "endangered". They are far too extraordinary to slip silently from our planet. "Wolves Forever" is our motto. It was suggested by Nick and we loved it.

## SCIENCE/MATH: Wolf Weigh-In

We had learned that the North American Gray Wolf weighed between 55 and 170 pounds. We decided to invite the school nurse and her big scale to come visit our class. We wanted to see how the weight of children compared to the weight of wolves. This could be approached in many ways. One child brought his dog to visit briefly on the "weigh-in" day in order for us to compare the weight of a German shepherd with a wolf. His dog weighed 70 pounds. We called a local veterinarian and found out that most German shepherds weigh between 60 and 80 pounds. Wolves could obviously be bigger than their domestic relatives! We decided to add up the total weight of all the children in our classroom to see how many 100-pound wolves could be represented. We invited the principal and discovered that not even he weighed as much as a large wolf! We posted our findings at our "Wolf Center."

## SCIENCE/MATH: A Wolf Island Clay Structure

We read the story *Wolf Island* by Celia Godkin (Freeman, 1993). We talked about what "the balance of nature" meant and how the wolf has an important job as a "predator." We created the story out of clay and also displayed it in our "Wolf Center."

## SOCIAL STUDIES:
## "Winter Wolf," a Video Story

We watched the wonderful video *Winter Wolf* which mixed Native American legend and real people to tell a magical kind of story. We thought again about how Indians respected the wolf, and yet even today it's still misunderstood. We added to a list we had been keeping at the "Wolf Center": Why Wolves Are Disliked.

## SOCIAL STUDIES:
## Wolf Communication
## (A Wolf Expert Speaks Out)

A lady from our local zoo really liked wolves and she taught us that wolves communicate in basically three ways: sounds, body language, and scents. She taught us that the position of the wolf's tail says many things. If a wolf is feeling aggressive, for example, it will puff up its tail and hold it up straight to make it look very big. As Earthkeepers, we were really interested in learning to read the signs of the wolf!

## Celebrations:
## A Howling Good Time on the Playground

We had learned a lot about wolves and what their various sounds and howls meant. People use different tones and volume of voice to express their feelings and so do wolves. In a book called *Discovering Wolves* by Nancy Field and Corliss Karasov (Dog-Eared Publications, 1992) there are many marvelous wolf facts, including a list of "Wolf Sounds." The children practiced howling sounds: "arr-rrr-rrr-oo-ooo" and "ow-oo-ow." Wolves have barking sounds: "Yip, yap, huff, and woof." Wolves also growl or whimper depending on the situation. On a warm winter day we went outside to the far end of the playground and had a howling good time being wolves. We weren't loud or silly. We listened as Helen gave us different situations and then asked us what sound we, as wolves, might use to respond. Wolves don't howl at the moon, but they howl for many other reasons—and so did we! We were learning to be good earth listeners and many of us hoped that one day we might be able to hear the howl of real wolves—wolves that would still be wild and free because we had learned to love and respect them when we were young. The class came back inside and gathered at the story stump to listen to *The Call of the Wolves* by Jim Murphy (Scholastic, 1989). This story of a young wolf in trouble had us all hoping it would be safe as we learned more about the real life problems wolves face.

## World Wondering:
## A Happy Howl-idays Card to World Earthkeepers

Near the end of our wolf study I read *A Wolf Story* by David McPhail (Scribners, 1981). We loved this story based on an actual incident that had taken place in London. It tells of a timber wolf, captured and taken from its home in the woods. It also relates the

success of a group of children in helping the wolf regain his freedom. It made us happy to know there are young and old people all over the world working in different ways to help save the wolf. Kelly (the little girl who had been so frightened a few weeks ago) suggested that we send cards to thank some of those "wolfkeepers"! We found a list of wolf organizations at the end of *The Eyes of the Gray Wolf*. We got busy making howl-iday cards to mail, thanking them for their good work. Kelly also asked if she could hold the class wolf. She was overheard talking to it softly, "I'm sorry they wrote all those mean stories about you. I'll tell my children the truth."

## Family Ties:
### Conducting Interviews and Creating a Newspaper

We had read *The True Story of the Three Little Pigs* by Jon Scieszka (Viking Kestrel, 1989). In this tale the wolf says he's been framed and is trying to set the story straight in the newspapers. We thought we'd help out with a little wolf truth. Each child interviewed an adult, asking how he felt about wolves. We published the responses and our favorite wolf facts in a class paper, *The Wolf Call*. We promised ourselves to be mindful of our goals as Earthkeepers to continue to learn and be curious about wolves. As we did so, we felt the wolves of the world were probably howling for joy somewhere wild on the planet!

# Books about Wolves

**Brett, Jan**. *The First Dog*. Harcourt Brace, New York, 1988.

**Bushnell, Jack**. *Circus of the Wolves*. Lothrop, Lee & Shepard, New York, 1994.

**Delaney, A.** *The Gunnywolf*. Harper and Row, New York, 1988.

**de Marolles, Chantal**. *The Lonely Wolf*. North-South Bks., New York, 1979.

**Scieszka, Jon**. *The True Story of the Three Little Pigs*. Penguin, New York, 1989.

**Gibbons, Gail**. *Wolves*. Holiday House, New York, 1994.

**Godkin, Celia**. *Wolf Island*. W.H. Freeman, New York, 1993.

**Green, Carol**. *Reading About the Gray Wolf*. Enslow Pub., Hillside, New Jersey, 1993.

**Harper, Wilhelmina**. *The Gunniwolf*. E.P.Dutton, New York, 1967.

**Kasza, Keiko**. *The Wolf's Chicken Stew*. G.P. Putnam's Sons, New York, 1987.

**Lawrence, R.D.** *Wolves*. Sierra Club Books, San Francisco, 1990.

**Ling, Mary**. *Amazing Wolves, Dogs, and Foxes*. Alfred A. Knopf, New York, 1991.

**Locker, Thomas**. *The Land of Gray Wolf*. Dial Books, New York, 1991.

**London, Jonathan**. *The Eyes of Gray Wolf*. Chronicle Books, San Francisco, 1993.

**Milton, Joyce**. *Wild, Wild Wolves*. Random House, New York, 1992.

**Murphy, Jim**. *The Call of the Wolves*. Scholastic, New York, 1989.

**Nickl, Peter**. *The Story of the Kind Wolf*. Henry Holt and Co., Inc., New York, 1982.

**Offen, Hilda**. *Nice Work, Little Wolf!* Dutton, New York, 1991.

**Powell, Mary**. *Wolf Tales: Native American Children's Stories*. Ancient City Press, Sante Fe, New Mexico, 1992.

**Prescott, Lyle**. "What's Up Pup?". Ranger Rick. National Wildlife Federation. 8925 Leesburg Pike, Vienna, Virginia. 22184-0001. Vol. 28, No. 7, July, 1994.

**Scieszka, Jon**. *The True Story of the Three Little Pigs*. Penguin, New York, 1989.

**Simon, Seymour**. *Wolves*. HarperCollins, New York, 1993.

**Trivias, Eugene**. *The Three Little Wolves and the Big Bad Pig*. Margaret McElderry Books, New York, 1993.

**Wolpert, Tom**. *Wolves for Kids*. NorthWord Press, Inc., Minocqua, Wisconsin, 1990.

## VIDEO

*Winter Wolf*. (VHS). Miramar, 200 Second Ave. W., Seattle, Washington 98119.

## FOR MORE INFORMATION

Write to Defenders of Wildlife, 1101 Fourteenth St., NW Suite 1400, Washington, DC 20005.

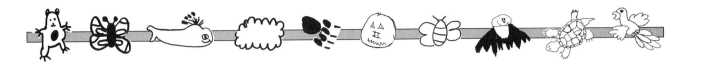

# The Wonder of Winter

*"Down came the dry flakes, fat enough and
heavy enough to crash like nickels on stone.
It always surprised him, how quiet it was.
Not like rain, but like a secret."*

—*Toni Morrison*

Winter had now come full force to the earth with a different kind of wonder! The months of winter are filled with fantastic opportunities for curious Earthkeepers. There is so much to observe, to record, to predict, to measure, and to wonder about! So we got ready to experiment, to read, to write, and to celebrate the layered beauty of the earth while beginning to unravel some of the mysteries behind her secrets.

## Earth Minute:

### Watching a Snow Storm

One day the wind was really howling outside the classroom, and snow was falling so thickly we couldn't even see the bird feeder by the window. It was exciting as we marveled at the power of nature to produce such a storm. We used this moment to do some serious winter wondering.

We read *Winter Harvest* by Jane Chelsea Aragon (Little, Brown, 1988), a story about a family feeding deer on a stormy winter day.

We ate apples like the deer in *Winter Harvest*, sipped hot cocoa, and turned off the lights while watching the snow and listening to the wind.

We wondered about snowflakes. How are they formed? Is each one really different? How could we find out?

We read winter poems, including "Snowflake," a favorite from *Earth Verses and Water Rhymes* by J. Patrick Lewis about a boy catching a snowflake on his tongue. Nathan remarked, "That's a good reason to keep the earth's water clean—so it will always be safe to catch snowflakes on our tongues!"

We wrote snow poems. Shemeka made her words go down the page like falling snow. There were many times during winter when we took time to watch and listen to the earth. You don't have to wait for a snowstorm to discover the wonders of winter in your classroom. Other ways to introduce winter include:

- **A Winter Chart.** We made a "Winter Is Coming" temperature chart-graph, following a discussion about signs of

# Did You Know?
## WINTER FACTS

- ○ Some animals change color in winter. Just the tip of the weasel's tail stays black. The snowshoe rabbit turns pure white.

- ○ Many insects spend the winter inside the bark of trees.

- ○ Many animals can fly to warmer places. Animals that do not migrate grow a winter coat and some hibernate in protected places.

- ○ No two snowflakes are exactly alike, even though every snowflake is a six-sided crystal.

- ○ A heavy snowfall will often clean the air of pollution.

- ○ Ten centimeters (four inches) of snow melts down to about one centimeter (0.4 inches) of water.

- ○ The stars are easier to see in winter because there is no haze or fog in the air.

- ○ In cold climates, lakes freeze over with a coating of ice, which may be more than a foot thick if it is cold enough. The ice is always at the top because solid water (ice) weighs less than liquid water.

- ○ In very cold places, such as Wisconsin, Minnesota, and Canada, the ice can be so thick people walk and drive snowmobiles and cars onto it.

- ○ When water freezes in the cracks of a rock or in a road, it expands and takes up more space. This causes rocks and roads to break up. This is why roads have potholes after the ice melts in the spring.

winter and the changing earth. We took turns being the meteorologist reporting to the class as we observed the weather patterns and anxiously awaited changes.

- **A winter's coming book.** We read *Goodbye Geese* and drew pictures about "what winter looks like" when it comes.

- **A classroom paper snowman.** Even on clear days, one can begin to think "snow." We shared *Mousekin's Frosty Friend* by Edna Miller (Simon and Schuster, 1990), a charming tale of a tiny mouse and his first encounter with a snowman. We attempted to determine the size of the snowman by careful observation of visual clues in the book. We then created a classroom paper snowman and other snow creatures and compared, measured, and charted their sizes and other characteristics.

- **"No-snow survey."** We conducted a world-without-snow survey. We listed all the things we could not do in a world where snow never fell. Children in "no-snow" areas of the country could list the advantages of living someplace where it never snows. They could then write about "The First Thing I Would do If It Snowed Tomorrow." It also can be fun to make a silent snowstorm. Take cotton balls. Present one to each child,

pretending it is a snowflake. Tell them that by working together you can create a snowstorm! On the count of three, all toss your "snowflake" up into the air. After the laughter and fun, return each flake to a "snow box" for another day. (This avoids losing the magic of the moment by not having a room full of graying cottonballs!)

# Literature Connections:

## Teaching with Books About Winter

One day in early winter, we read Charlotte Zolotow's *Something Is Going to Happen* (HarperCollins, 1993). Every member of the family, even the dog, awakens one day with the same feeling: Something is going to happen! The day passes, the feeling persists. At last they open the door and see: "Slowly drifting through the air were thousands of white ice flakes. They had settled on the ground and covered the world with white.

You can imagine our delight the next morning when we awoke to a snow-covered earth. We decided to begin a Winter Book Fest and read lots of great winter books over the next few days while the snow hung on.

- *Owl Moon* by Jane Yolen (Philomel, 1987). In this gentle book, a father and child set out one winter night to look for owls. After sharing the story we bundled up and took a listening walk. Instead of talking about what we saw along the way, we returned to the classroom and used the information we gathered by careful observation to create a picture story.

- Another wonderful walk is taken by a mother and child in *A Winter Walk* by Lynne Barasch (Ticknor and Fields, 1993). The two look closely and together "see" all the many colors of winter. Then we read *White Wonderful Winter!* by Elaine

Good (Good Books, 1991) and had a great discussion about what winter looks like. We created "The Color of Winter" poems and displayed them with a color border that matched the color that each one of us chose.

- *The Snow Speaks* by Nancy White Carlstorm (Little, Brown, 1992) speaks enticingly of the wonders of the first snow, as she says "The children know if they use their wise and patient eyes, they can read other secrets of the snow." What a good book for young Earthkeepers who are learning to listen and look carefully! The story considers the many different ways "the snow speaks." We shared ways the snow "speaks" for us!

- *The Mitten* by Jan Brett (Scholastic, 1989) and *The Mitten* by Alvin Tresselt (Scholastic, 1964) are two adaptations of an old Ukranian folktale in which animals take refuge in a lost mitten. After reading both versions we created Venn diagrams comparing the two stories. We sorted mittens, measured mittens, and wrote our own versions of the story, creating new endings. We read together other similar stories such as *The Mystery of the Missing Red Mitten* by Steven Kellogg and *Runaway Mittens* by Jean Rogers (Greenwillow, 1988). Again, we went to the map to see where these stories took place.

# Integrating the Idea:

## LANGUAGE ARTS: Snow Secrets

On the poetry board I wrote these words:

*"Down came the dry flakes, fat enough and heavy enough to crash like nickels on stone. It always surprised him, how quiet it was. Not like rain, but like a secret."*
—Toni Morrison

We read these words together and talked about how they made us feel happy and peaceful! Then I read the preface poem, *White Snow, Bright Snow* by Alvin Tresselt (Scholastic, 1977).

It was also filled with pretty words: "Softly, gently in the secret night, Down from the North came the quiet white...." We talked about how snow can be like a "secret." "It's quiet!" said Nick.

We talked about what other kinds of things could be as quiet as a secret. "A careful Earthkeeper wanting to see a deer in the forest!" suggested Nathan.

We had lots of ideas, but we tried to choose our favorite winter word and then write it on a snowflake cutout. We hung these up near the windows where we could see the real snowflakes continuing to fall! We loved the feel of "winter words"!

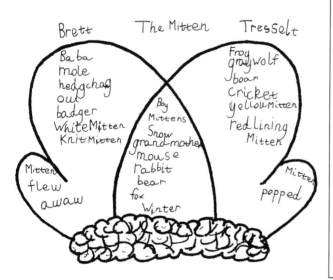

## LANGUAGE ARTS:
## Poetry Break

We used those words to inspire more poems about our observations of "earth changes" during this frosty, wonderful weather.

To find out what other poets have to say about the season we read *It's Snowing! It's Snowing!* by Jack Prelutsky (Greenwillow, 1984) and winter poems by other authors in *Sing a Song of Popcorn* (Scholastic, 1988).

---

Winter Time
by Kate

In winter time cheeks get rosy red
In winter time kids have fun
In winter time the snow flakes fall
While moms tuck kids into bed.

---

Winter    By Sophia

I like winter
My Birthday's in it

I like winter
The Snow won'st quit it.
I love winter
I can go sledding
I like winter
Because it's funny

---

In Winter time the Wind Does blow And the ground is All covered With snow. But When spring is here and Summer grows near, I can Wait For the cold Next year.

```
W  inters  wondrful
I  cy
N  ice
T  erific
E  xullent
R  elly  remarkuble
```

## MATH/SCIENCE:
## Animals in Winter

Where we live, temperatures drop during the winter. One really cold day, Helen led a discussion of questions like: "How do you stay warm in winter? What changes do you make in your clothing and in your activities?" Then she asked, "How do animals adapt?" She wrote down the answers, and all decided to investigate further to learn where insects, reptiles, mammals, birds, and other animals go in the winter.

- **Becoming a chipmunk.** I visited the classroom for a story sesssion one fall day. I called the children to the story stump and picked up the *Chipmunk Song* by Joanne Ryder (Lodestar, 1987). I gave each child an acorn to hold carefully in his or her hand. In our imaginations, we transformed into tiny chipmunks to experience a journey into hibernation. We had fun.

- **More books.** We read other great books, like *Every Autumn Comes the Bear* by James Arnosky (Putnam, 1993), *Winter* by Ron Hirschi (Cobblehill, 1990), and *Keep Looking* by Millicent Selsam and Joyce Hunt (Macmillan, 1989).

- **A winter mural.** After our research was done, children collaborated on murals that showed how animals live during different seasons.

## MATH/SCIENCE:
## Snow Sculpture

We built two snowmen outside (one large and one small). We recorded daily temperatures and log predictions in a "Day in the Life of Our Snowman" journal. We watched the video, *The Snowman*, based on the book by Raymond Briggs about a fantastic snowman that came to life.

## SOCIAL STUDIES:
## Winter Across the Earth

A trip across time zones: we read *Nine O'Clock Lullaby* by Marilyn Singer (Harper Collins, 1991), a rhythmic tale that took us on a trip across different time zones all over the world. We wondered how winter and weather were different in all those places. We read *All Dressed Up and Nowhere to Go* by Daniel Joseph and Lydia Mendel (Houghton Mifflin, 1993). In this story, David visits his grandparents in Florida where he dreams about making a snowman just like the ones he made in Maine. It quickly becomes apparent that winter is very different on different parts of the planet. David ends up making a "sandman."

- **Snowman or Sandman game.** We invented a game! We each had made a "Snowman" and "Sandman" card. One player points to a spot on the globe. The others can hold up the card they think is appropriate. Interesting geography discussion emerged from this game!

- **Warm water won't freeze!** We read *Midnight Snowman* by Caroline Feller Bauer (Atheneum, 1957) then discussed how geography affects the capability of water to be transformed into a flake of snow. We each chose a particular place on the planet. "Finish this sentence," said Helen—"If I were a snowflake falling here on the earth I would...." Our stories were assembled into a "Tale of Snowflakes" book. After reading *In Snowflakes, Sugar and Salt* by Chu Maki (Lerner, 1993), we looked at real snowflakes. They were beautiful!

- **Dirty air—Dirty snow!** Dirty air, however, makes for dirty snow. I discussed with the children the snow ice cream I had made as a child with my mother. Now, however, I wasn't certain the air was clean enough for us to eat snow that had fallen through it. Interesting discussions happened. (E.G., why is the air dirty?)

## SOCIAL STUDIES: Winters Past

- **Picture of a winter memory.** It was fun wondering about winters past! The children had only been alive for a few winters, but already each had unique favorite winter memories. Each drew a picture of "My Most Wonderful Winter Moment." We shared these memories and read the book *Snowed In* by Barbara Lucas (Bradbury, 1993). This lovely book tells the tale of a family in 1915 that is unable to leave their home all winter because of the heavy snows. We were fascinated with the way the time was filled for these snowbound children. We invited older members of our families to come and share a favorite winter memory.

- **Writing memory letters.** We read *Dear Rebecca, Winter Is Here* by Jean Craighead George (HarperCollins, 1993), a book full of lovely winter observations made by a grandmother and documented in a letter to her granddaughter. We wrote to relatives, asking each to share a favorite winter memory. We displayed these letters with our winter pictures.

Dear First Grade Parents,

One very important part of learning about wise stewardship of the earth's wonderful resources is understanding the concept of "reuse." We have been discussing the different choices we can make when we no longer need an item. We can throw it away, which wastes the earth's resources, or we can share it with someone else. We decided the latter was a smart way to help save the earth.

We then discussed items that each one of us might have that we no longer need. Mittens were one of the first items to come to our minds, as we have been learning about the "Wonder of Winter" and reading two different versions of the Ukranian folktale, "The Mitten". We shared together how fortunate we are that our hands have been warm and that we have enough mittens, scarves, coats, and other warm clothing.

One of our first graders suggested creating a "Mitten Tree." We could collect used and new mittens to give to children who are in need of their winter warmth. We would like to encourage you to look with your child for mittens that he/she has outgrown or no longer needs and bring them to school to hang on our tree. We understand that during these cold months there is a desperate need in our community for warm clothing, especially for children. We will place a container under our Mitten Tree for larger winter items. We'll be accepting donations to our Mitten Tree through mid-January.

Thank you for your participation in this project. Together we work to become good stewards of the earth!

# Earth Minute:

## A Mitten Tree and a Visit from Mother Earth

As we thought about all the gifts we get from earth, we wondered how we could help save those gifts. We decided to invite our families to join us in reusing earth's great gifts and helping people at the same time. We sent a letter home explaining our projects.

## Mother Earth Surprises Us!

Mother Earth (really me, in disguise) visited to accept the students' gifts of reusable resources. I presented the children with a tiny "Precious Things" basket and asked them to choose something special from the earth to keep in their baskets forever. (One child was so exited, his mom reported, that he cleaned and rearranged his entire room to find the perfect spot for his basket!) We wrote a song to share with the guests who were coming to accept our gifts of mittens and to give them to other children to warm their hands.

*Thanks for warm*
*hands and thanks*
*for warm hearts.*
*Thanks for the chance*
*for us to do our part.*
*If we all work, we can*
*help and can share.*
*And make life better*
*for children everywhere.*
*Love brings us all together.*

We were still celebrating the results of our Mitten Tree! As the winter holidays approached, we explored more activities to Celebrate the Earth and this time of giving.

- **If I were a gift.** We thought about giving a gift to earth. "If I were a gift to earth, I would be ...." We shared ideas on a bulletin board.

- **Gifts from Earth.** We brainstormed about gifts we could give that respect the earth. One idea was student-made clay pots filled with forest potpourri, wrapped in recycled paper or hand-decorated brown paper bags.

- **Gifts for Earth.** We coated pine cones with peanut butter, rolled them in bird seed, and attached twine ties to make bird-feeders. We kept bird-watching journals about our new friends.

# Books about Winter

**Aragon, Jane Chelsea.** *Winter Harvest.* Little, Brown, Boston, 1988.

**Barasch, Lynn.** *A Winter Walk.* Ticknor and Fields, New York, 1993.

**Bauer, Caroline.** *Midnight Snowman.* Macmillan, New York, 1987.

**Brett, Jan.** *The Mitten.* Scholastic, New York, 1989.

**Bunting, Eve.** *Night Tree.* Harcourt Brace Jovanovich, New York, 1991.

**Butterworth, Nick.** *One Snowy Night.* Little, Brown, Boston, 1989.

**Carlstrom, Nancy White.** *The Snow Speaks.* Little, Brown, Boston, 1992.

**Dunphy, Madeleine.** *Here is the Arctic Winter.* Hyperion, New York, 1993.

**George, Jean Craighead.** *Dear Rebecca, Winter Is Here.* HarperCollins, New York, 1993.

**Good, Elaine.** *White Wonderful Winter!.* Good Books, Intercourse, Pennsylvania, 1991.

**Hader, Berta,** and **Elma Hader.** *The Big Snow.* Aladdin, Macmillan, New York, 1988.

**Hirschi, Ron.** *Winter.* Cobblehill, New York, 1990.

**Hissey, Jane.** *Jolly Snow: An Old Bear Story.* Philomel, New York, 1991.

**Joseph, Daniel M.** and **Lydia J. Mendel.** *All Dressed Up and Nowhere to Go.* Houghton Mifflin, Boston, 1993.

**Kellogg, Steven.** *The Mystery of the Missing Red Mitten.* Greenwillow, New York, 1988.

**Keown, Elizabeth.** *Emily's Snowball: The World's Biggest.* Antheneum, New York, 1992.

**Lewis, Kim.** *First Snow.* Candlewick, Massachusetts, 1993.

**Lockwood, Primrose,** and **Elaine Mills.** *One Winter.* Cobblehill, New York, 1990.

**Lotz, Karen E.** *Snowsong Whistling.* Dutton, New York, 1993.

**Lucas, Barbara M.** *Snowed In.* Bradbury, New York, 1993.

**Maass, Robert.** *When Winter Comes.* Henry Holt, New York, 1993.

**Maki, Chu.** *Snowflakes, Sugar, and Salt.* Lerner, Minneapolis, 1993.

**Mendez, Phil.** *The Black Snowman.* Scholastic, New York, 1989.

**Miller, Edna.** *Mousekin's Frosty Friend.* Simon and Schuster, New York, 1990.

**Parnall, Peter.** *Winter Barn.* Macmillan, New York, 1986.

**Rogers, Jean.** *Runaway Mittens.* Greenwillow, New York, 1988.

**San Souci, Daniel.** *North Country Night.* Doubleday, New York, 1990.

**Singer, Marilyn.** *Nine O'Clock Lullaby.* HarperCollins, New York, 1991.

**Tresselt, Alvin.** *The Mitten.* Scholastic, New York, 1964.

**Tresselt, Alvin.** *White Snow Bright Snow.* Scholastic, New York, 1947.

**Warnok, Natalie Kinsey.** *When Spring Comes.* Dutton, New York, 1994.

**Willard, Nancy.** *A Starlit Somersault Downhill.* Little, Brown, Boston, 1993.

**Yolen, Jane.** *Owl Moon.* Scholastic, New York, 1987.

**Zolotow, Charlotte.** *Something Is Going to Happen.* Harper and Row, New York, 1988.

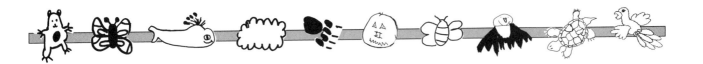

# For the Love of Whales

*"These whales—How can we help but love them!"*
—The Gift of the Whales

The beauty and wonder of whales have captivated human imagination for centuries. Whales have lived peacefully on the planet for millions of years. Then about 2,000 years ago man began to hunt them. By 1900 many whales had been forced to the brink of extinction. However, in recent years with the development of alternatives to the products provided by the whale, the beleaguered giant seems to have been given a second chance. It is now protected to varying degrees, and as we begin to look at the whale as a fellow traveler on the planet rather than merely a product for human consumption, we are struck anew with its magnificence! The whale was to be our Animal of the Month, culminating our study of water. What a grand finale!

planet," I said. A silence fell over the room as we listened intently. Soon the soft sounds of the ocean could be heard! "Now open your eyes. I want to share a story with you about one of the grandest animals ever to live in the ocean. Listen carefully, for this creature is to be our new Animal of the Month," I said, and then shared the magnificently illustrated *The Whale's Song* by Dyan Sheldon (Dial 1990). In this story a little girl named Lilly is told a wondrous tale of whales. Her grandmother relates to Lilly how once long ago, she had given the whales a gift and the whales in return had given her the gift of their song! Lilly then decides to give the whales a gift too, in the hope that she too will hear the song of the whales. The children in the classroom sat enraptured as I pulled a yellow

## Earth Minute:

### Listening for the Whale's Song!

I came to the room and called out "Earth Break!" We gathered at the story stump. "Close your eyes and listen with your best earthkeeper ears and raise your hand quietly when you hear a new, special sound of the

## Did You Know?
## WHALE FACTS

○ The blue whale is the largest living animal on earth. It can grow to over 100 feet in length and weigh nearly 390,000 pounds. The life span is about 100 years.

○ There are 77 types of whales: ten species of baleen and 67 species of toothed whales.

○ Breaching occurs when a whale leaps into the air, twists its body around, and crashes back into the water on its back.

○ Whale mothers like to have their babies stay close. Whales have one calf at a time.

○ A whale's flipper is made up of five bones that look like fingers.

○ Male humpback whales can sing much like songbirds, with repeating patterns.

○ When a baby humpback calf is born it is as big as a car.

○ Whales often travel in small groups of three or more, called pods.

○ Dolphins and porpoises are small, toothed whales.

○ Orca or killer whales are highly cooperative and social. They hunt in packs like wolves. They feed not on krill, but on a variety of creatures, from birds to seals.

○ A blue whale calf gains nearly 180 pounds a day.

○ The blue whale is endangered. Since 1967 it could no longer be hunted, but by then its numbers had already been reduced to 14,000 from around 300,000.

○ Whales were hunted for their oil and baleen. Today alternatives have been found for all products except whale meat, which is an expensive gourmet food item in some countries.

○ The whale has no enemies except man.

flower from my pocket and let it fall to the floor, as I read the words from the story explaining how Lilly had pulled a yellow flower from her pocket and dropped it into the ocean calling to the air, "This is for you!" At the story's end, the whales do come to Lilly and she hears them calling her name in a magical conclusion. As the sound of the ocean (on tape) continued, the story ended, and our study of whales began! We loved the book and wrote about "If I were to give a gift to the whales."

# Literature Connections:

## Teaching with Books about Whales

We read two wonderful fiction stories about whales, which had some "real" whale facts in them. We read *Mr. Friend Whale* by Simon James (A Bantam Little Rooster Book, 1990) and *Dear Mr. Blueberry* also by Simon James (McElderry Books, 1991.)

● **A comparison chart:** We recorded how these stories were alike and different.

● **A great whales fact list:** We sorted out what was fact and fiction and began a list.

● **Fact bubbles:** We had a "Great Whale" bulletin board in the hallway and made fact bubbles coming out of the water spout. Children could add a bubble whenever they learned a new fact. There were lots of interesting facts at the end of *My Whale Friend*, but some of them made us angry, like the one that said more than two million whales have been killed in the last fifty years and that some whales have been hurt so badly they might die out altogether!

# Integrating the Idea:

## LANGUAGE ARTS:
## Whale Reports

We know that as good earthkeepers the best thing we can do for whales is to become "whale-smart," so we will be well-informed earthkeepers on their behalf.

**Attribute research:** We decided to do some research on the different characteristics of whales. Books like *Whales* by Gail Gibbons (Holiday House, 1991) gave us lots of information.

- **Group reports:** We broke into groups to read and research more about six different species of whales, like the blue, beluga, orca, and narwhal. We made web charts looking for information such as food, habitat, physical characteristics, enemies, and communication techniques of our particular whale. When we were all done we shared our information. Earthkeepers know how important it is to work together and share the load!

- **A whale watcher's bulletin board:** As earthkeepers we wanted to tell others about what we were learning. We kept adding reports and drawings and fact bubbles to our bulletin board in the hallway so that everyone could share our findings.

Gray Whale

## LANGUAGE ARTS:
## A Whale Tale Message

We had learned that the markings on the whales' flukes are like finger prints. They are different for each humpback. We decided to design our own individual whale tail including a message for the earth in our design!

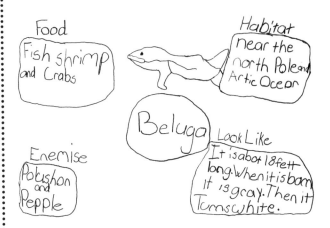

Food
Fish shrimp and Crabs

Habitat
near the north Pole and Arctic Ocean

Beluga

Enemise
Polushon and Pepple

Look Like
It is abot 18 fett long. When it is born it is gray. Then it Turns white.

## SCIENCE/MATH:
## Visualizing Vastness

We learned that a blue whale can be as large as 25 to 30 elephants, so we made an elephant pattern and cut out 30 elephants and then drew a whale around them, to help us imagine the size. We also knew that the blue whale can be 100 feet long. We went outside to try to make the outline of a whale. It's so large, we didn't even have enough people in our class to outline the bottom of the whale. We watched a great video, *Sizing Up Animals*, which gave us lots of tips about how to understand animal sizes.

Save The Whales, Butrfizes and The Earth.

A Whale's Tale

71

## SCIENCE/MATH: Can-Counting Culmination/ 1,000 Cans!

Weeks ago, during our water unit, we began collecting and counting cans to recycle. The children knew we were going to do something special with the money we earned. Now we were excited to learn what that was! We were going to protect a whale! Not in our classroom of course, but one roaming free and safe in the seas. We chose one named Bat. This was special to us since we had learned so many wonderful things about bats earlier in the year, and now we were the care-takers of an "ocean-flying bat"! We celebrated when we were able to record the 1,000th can on our chart. We had met our goal. We sent off our hard-earned money and waited for the picture of Bat to arrive in the mail. We were glad we had helped the earth by recycling all those aluminum cans, too! We were learning about the power of good choices.

## SCIENCE/MATH: Habitat Dioramas and Dilemmas

● **A guest shared a great whale story:** Kahla, a fourth grade friend, came to read the story of *Humphrey: The Lost Whale*, by Wendy Tokuda and Richard Hall (Heian International, Inc., 1986). We were learning, through stories like this one, about the problems faced by the great whales. Kahla made "Save the Whale" bookmarks for each of us, and brought a shoebox habitat she had made. She agreed to come back another day and help us create our own "Ocean Home Dioramas." We were really beginning to think about how important it is to keep the ocean waters clean and safe!

● **Oil spill in a jar:** Another guest earthkeeper shared the story of *Ibis: A True Whale Story*, by John Himmelman (Scholastic, 1990). Ibis is caught in a fisherman's net and gets in real trouble! "Just imagine," said our guest, "that Ibis might also be caught in an oil spill." To help us, she took a glass jar of water and poured oil into it. We could see clearly as oil reached down into the water and then returned to float on the top. She then took a series of items and dipped them into the "oil slick." We could see the awful damage! A white feather became brown and slimy and lifeless looking. As the guest raised a beautiful white sand dollar to place in the "slick" all the students cried out "No!" The guest poised her hand and said, "If you will try to always remember your Earthkeeper goals and to be curious about whales and the waters they swim, I will spare this lovely sand dollar!" All the children eagerly agreed. The oil slick was placed in our whale center and gave us much to think about.

## SOCIAL STUDIES: "My Whale Brother" — Whales in Native American Culture

- **A whale video:** We watched *Gift of the Whales* in which Dan Hunter, a Native American from Alaska comes to respect and love the whales as he listens to the ancient wisdom of his grandfather and the modern-day wisdom of a wild life biologist. He learns he too wants to be a friend to the whales.

- **A whale folktale:** We read *Whale Brother* by Barbara Steiner (Walker, 1988) in which another young boy, Omu, discovers the wonder of these great creatures that are our brothers. Omu learns that good works take time and effort and love. Whales have much to teach us and were held in great respect by Native Americans.

# Celebrations:

## Our Whale Protection Effort Is Official

It finally came—our picture of Bat and the protection certificate! We celebrated by going on a whale watch after being officially inducted into the "Royal Order of the Whales!" Each child was presented a heart adorned with two whale stickers. As this paper medallion was placed around the child's neck, the teacher said respectfully, "For your efforts in helping the world's whales, you are now an official member of the Royal Order of the Whales." We read *Going on a Whale Watch* by Bruce McMillan (Scholastic, 1992.) We learned that on the ocean coasts people like to go out in boats

"whale watching." We decided to pretend we were in a boat on the Atlantic Ocean as we watched the video *Your Favorite Whale—Bat.* It featured real footage of the humpback we had adopted. It was great! We love you, Bat!

# World Wondering:

## Honoring a Whale Watcher

We read the story *The Whale in Lowell's Cove,* by Jane Robinson (Down East Books, 1992.) We thought a lot about the problems of this whale trapped in a cove in Maine and about Charlie Gillman, the kind fisherman who helped her. We made Charlie our Earth-keeper of the Month and wrote him letters of thanks. We knew we would be curious about whales all our lives but we were also earthkeepers and wanted to be certain that we always respected the need for whales to be wild and free. We celebrated when a student brought an article saying that the Antarctic was being set aside as a sanctuary for whales. This means they can't be hunted there! Perhaps the times are changing for real, and people who were once the whale's only enemy are now a protector and friend. May there always be whales on earth!

# Family Tie:

## A Whale of a Thank You!

We collected 1,000 aluminum cans to recycle for cash—which we used to adopt a whale. Parents transported the cans to the recycling center.

# Books about Whales

**Aliki.** *My Visit to the Aquarium.* HarperCollins, New York, 1993.

**Allen, Judy.** *Whale.* Candlewick Press, Cambridge, Massachusetts, 1992.

**Berger, Gilda.** *Whales.* Doubleday, Garden City, New York, 1987.

**Bright, Michael.** *Humpback Whale.* Gloucester Press, New York. 1989.

**Chapin, Tom.** *Sing a Whale Song.* Random House, New York, 1993.

**Cousteau Society.** *Whales.* Simon and Schuster, New York, 1993.

**D'Vincent, Cynthia.** *The Whale Family Book.* Verlag Neugebauer Press, Salzburg, 1992.

**Dow, Lesley.** *Whales.* Facts on File Incorporated, New York, 1990.

**Ellis, Richard Physty,** *The True Story of a Young Whale's Rescue.* Courage Books, Philadelphia, 1993.

**Gibbons, Gail.** *Whales.* Holiday House, New York, 1991.

**Greene, Carol.** *The Humpback Whale.* Enslow, Hillside, New Jersey, 1993.

**Himmelman, John.** *Ibis: A True Whale Story.* Scholastic, New York, 1990.

**Hirschi, Ron.** *Discover My World: Ocean.* Bantam, New York, 1991.

**Hulme, Joy N.** *Sea Squares.* Hyperion Books, New York, 1991.

**James, Simon.** *Dear Mr. Blueberry.* Margaret K. McElderry, New York, 1991.

**Johnston, Tony.** *Whale Song.* G. P. Putmam, New York, 1987.

**Knapp, Toni.** *The Six Bridges of Humphrey The Whale.* Rockrimmon Press, Colorado Springs, 1989.

**Lauber, Patricia.** *Great Whales: The Gentle Giants.* Henry Holt, New York, 1991.

**Livingston, Myra Cohn.** *If You Ever Meet a Whale.* Holiday House, New York, 1992.

**Marshak, Suzanna.** *I Am the Ocean.* Arcade, New York, 1992.

**McGovern, Ann.** *Little Whale.* Scholastic, New York, 1979.

**McMillan, Bruce.** *Going On a Whale Watch.* Scholastic, New York, 1992.

**Nobisso, Josephine.** *Shh! The Whale Is Smiling.* Simon and Schuster, New York,1992.

**Papastavrou, Vassili.** *Whales and Dolphins.* Bookwright Press, New York, 1991.

**Patent, Dorothy Hinshaw.** *Killer Whales.* Holiday House, New York, 1993.

**Penny, Malcolm.** *Let's Look at Whales.* Bookwright Press. New York, 1990.

**Petty, Kate.** *Whales.* Gloucester Press, New York, 1988.

**Ryder, Joanne.** *Winter Whale.* Morrow Junior Books, New York, 1991.

**Sheldon, Dyan.** *The Whale's Song.* Dial Books, New York, 1990.

**Simon, Seymour.** *Whales.* Harper Collins, New York, 1989.

**Sis, Peter.** *An Ocean World.* Greenwillow Books, New York, 1992.

**Smyth, Karen C.** *Crystal: The Story of a Real Baby Whale.* Down East Books, Camden, Maine, 1986.

**Steele, Phillip.** *The Blue Whale.* Kingfisher, New York, 1994.

**Steiner, Barbara.** *Whale Brother.* Walker and Company, New York, 1988.

**Tokuda, Wendy,** and **Richard Hall.** *Humphrey the Lost Whale.* Heian International, Union City, California, 1986.

**Weller, Frances Ward.** *I Wonder If I'll See*

*a Whale.* Philomel Books, New York, 1991.

**Wilson, Lynn**. *Baby Whale.* Platt and Munk, New York, 1991.

**Wolpert, Tom.** *Whales for Kids.* NorthWord Press, Minocqua, Wisconsin, 1990.

**Ziefert, Harriet.** *Henry's Wrong Turn.* Little, Brown and Company, Boston, 1989.

## VIDEOS

*Dolphins and Orcas.* Bob Talbot, P.O. Box 3126 Rancho Palos Verdes, California 90274.

*Gift of the Whales.* Miramar Images. 200 Second Avenue West, Seattle, Washington, 98119.

*Portrait of a Whale.* National Geographic Society, Washington, D.C. 20036.

*Sizing Up Animals.* National Geographic Society, Washington, D.C. 20036.

*Watching the Whales*, Marine Mammal Fund. Fort Mason Center, Bldg. E, San Francisco, California 94123.

## WHALE PROTECTION PROJECT

International Wildlife Coalition, 70 E Falmouth Highway, East Falmouth, Massachusetts 02556-0388.

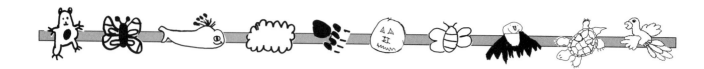

# The Wonder of Air

*"Down through the good air that holds us,*
*Flying like birds to the nest,*
*Let the warm darkness enfold us.*
*Fly to the earth and then rest!"*

—Reeve Lindbergh

## Earth Minute:

### Taking a Deep Breath

It was time for another Earth Minute as we began to explore yet another marvel of our planet—the atmosphere! I went to the story stump and sat down with an Earth bag. Inside the bag, Helen promised, was one of the most important things on Earth! The children tried to guess what it might be. They asked questions and attempted to solve yet another earth mystery. "Yes, it was something we all liked. No, it wasn't green." (Well, at least most of the time!) Finally, I opened the bag and asked Nathan to come look and report his Earthkeeper observation. He peered carefully for a long time, then he looked up at me and grinned and said, "This is like the fish tank, isn't it, Mrs. Dee?! There's nothing in it." I assured him that it was not like the fish tank incident of several months ago and that indeed there was something very important in the bag. Still he didn't know what it might be. I had him come up and sit on the story stump. Then I asked him to hold his breath for as long as he could. Of course, we all loved observing his efforts to hold his breath! "Now breathe," I said, and he gulped in a huge breath of air. "Now what did you breathe into your body, Nathan?" I asked.

"Air!" he replied. "Oh! I get it, Mrs. Dee! There is air in your bag!" And so began the journey that Helen would take with her class into one of the true miracles of our planet—the blanket of air that surrounds it and on which all of our lives depend!

Air, like water, is so important to our lives and we don't think about it much, because it has always been there for us. We decided to think more about it!

- **Clean air search.** We went home and did a "Clean Air Search." We looked in our own homes for things that could pollute

the air—things like mothballs, paint, oil, etc. Students took a note home to their parents asking them to search with their child. They were not to do it alone! Some of these materials we learned could be dangerous. It was interesting to look for the "bad air guys" with the help of parents. We began to think about more choices we could make for clean air. We talked about riding bikes, carpooling, or walking to places. The exercise would be good for our bodies, and walking doesn't pollute the earth!

- **Clean air detectors**. We made clean air detectors. We took pieces of paper, designed earths on them and called them our "Clean Air Detectors." We put a thin layer of petroleum jelly on them and placed them in the room and outside for a week. We brought them back in for examination with a magnifying glass and could really see the "particles" that are carried in the air as they lay trapped in our clean air detectors.

This planet is mine.

# Literature Connections:

## A Celebration of Air

- **We tried to think of ways to "see" air.** We went out onto the playground where we blew bubbles, tested pinwheels for wind, and flew a kite. Air really is

## *Did You Know?* AIR FACTS

- Air is a mixture of invisible gases— mainly nitrogen and oxygen.
- The layer of air around the earth is called the atmosphere. It acts like a blanket and helps keep the earth warm.
- Air brings weather and its changes.
- Moving air is called wind.
- Warm air rises and cold air sinks.
- Birds glide on warm air "rivers."
- The hottest recorded air temperature on Earth was 136 degrees in the Sahara Desert in 1922.

everywhere. We wrote poems about it!

- **Air books.** We again dove into good books and imaginative stories about air. We always made sure we knew what was fact and what was fiction.

- **Properties of air.** We learned about the properties of air, through science experiments just as we had done with water. It is colorless, and expands and contracts, and rises and falls!

● **Guest air experts!** We also had two wonderful air experts come and visit the classroom. They showed us that hot air rises and those currents can also make things move. We began to see that temperature of the air can make winds happen. Our most interesting experiment was taking an old cloth and putting it over the tail pipe of a car and starting the motor. We watched as Rick did this. Wow! Were we ever surprised when he brought the cloth in and opened it up for us! It was so dirty! We discussed how cars produce particles that get into the air and make it dirty. Rick asked us how we would like to breathe air that was full of the black particles on the cloth. None of us liked that idea and we began to discuss things that we could do to cut down on air pollution!

# Books about Air

**Bacon, Ron.** *Wind.* Scholastic, New York, 1984.

**Baines, John.** *Conserving the Atmosphere.* Steck-Vaughn, Austin, Texas, 1990.

**Branley, Franklyn.** *Oxygen Keeps You Alive.* Thomas Crowell, New York, 1971.

**Butterworth, Nick.** *One Blowy Night.* Little, Brown, Canada, 1992.

**Carlstrom, Nancy White.** *How Does the Wind Walk?* Macmillan, New York, 1993.

**de Paola, Tommie.** *Michael Bird-Boy.* Prentice Hall, New York, 1987.

**Dewey, Ariane.** *The Sky.* Green Tiger, New York, 1993.

**Edom, Helen.** *Science With Air.* EDC, Tulsa, Oklahoma, 1991.

**Gerson, Mary-Joan.** *Why the Sky is Far Away: A Nigerian Folktale.* Little, Brown, Canada, 1992.

**Gibbons, Gail.** *Catch the Wind! All About Kites.* Little, Brown, New York, 1989.

**Haseley, Dennis.** *Kite Flier.* Macmillan, New York, 1993.

**Kalman, Bobbie,** and **Janine Schaub.** *The Air I Breathe.* Crabtree Pub., New York, 1993.

**Killion, Bette.** *The Same Wind.* HarperCollins, New York, 1992.

**Lindbergh, Reeve.** *View from the Air: Charles Lindbergh's Earth and Sky.* Viking, New York, 1992.

**Patchett, Lynne.** *Clean Air Dirty Air.* A & C Black, London, 1993.

**Richardson, Joy.** *Air.* Franklin Watts, New York, 1992.

**Schmid, Eleonore.** *The Air Around Us.* North-South, New York, 1992.

**Soutter-Perrot, Andrienne.** *Air.* American Education, New York, 1993.

**Stille, Darlene.** *Air Pollution.* A New True Book. Children's Press, Chicago, 1990.

**Stille, Darlene.** *The Ozone Hole.* A New True Book. Children's Press, Chicago, 1991.

**Suhr, Mandy.** *How I Breathe.* Carolrhoda, Minneapolis, 1992.

**Vaughn, Marcia.** *Where Does the Wind Go?* Scholastic, New York, 1984.

**Wheeler, Jill.** *The Air We Breathe.* Abdo and Daughters, Edina, 1990.

**Wiesner, David.** *Hurricane.* Clarion, New York, 1990.

**Zolotow, Charlotte.** *When the Wind Stops.* Abelard-Schuman, New York, 1962.

## AUDIOVISUAL

*Let's Clear the Air: Understanding Air Pollution.* An Audiovisual Presentation of the National WIldlife Federation. Washington, D.C.

*The Red Balloon: A Film by Alvert Lamorisse* (VHS). Nelson Entertainment, 335 North Maple Drive, Beverly Hills, California 90210.

## REFERENCES

**Baines, John.** *Conserving the Atmosphere.* Steck-Vaughn Library, Austin, Texas, 1989.

# For the Love of the Rainforest

*"What would the world be once bereft of wet and wildness?*
*Let them be left. O let them be left, wildness and wet..."*

—Gerald Manley Hopkins (1844-1889)

There exist on this planet pockets of emerald wonder so full of life that it is difficult to comprehend their complexity and majesty. There is no journey more exciting, however, than delving into the endless wonders of the world's rainforests! We had just finished our look at air. We knew trees provided us with life-giving oxygen, and here was a place so full of giant trees it has sometimes been called "the lungs of the planet."

Sadly, these treasure houses are in some trouble. When NASA took pictures of our earth from space, we saw for the first time, not only the breathtaking majesty of our blue planet, but also the smoke from the fires destroying the earth's rainforests! "Man is the only creature to defile his own nest," Jacques Cousteau once remarked. These forests were to be the final stop on our Animal of the Month journey. We had investigated individual animals previously. This time we would honor an "ecosystem" that was threatened, thus endangering all its inhabitants.

The animals of the Amazon rainforest were to be our focus of study as we learned about one of the most amazing ecosystems on the planet. Today we are all born global citizens and it is good to be curious about the whole earth! We can touch on the problems while exhilarating in the grandeur. And so our rainforest adventure begins.

## Earth Minute:

### Listening to a Tropical Treasure

When the children arrived at school one morning I had placed a green box covered with wondrous creatures by the story stump with a "Do not open yet" sign on it. I came in for an Earth Minute and asked the children to close their eyes and open their ears and imagine the wonderful place I was going to tell them about!

We soon heard amazing sounds of water, rain, wind, and the calls of many creatures. We imagined that we were standing in a place that was wet and warm with trees that stood as tall as a ten story building. Green, tangled vines have bright flowers that look like jewels glistening in the forest. Butterflies and birds fly everywhere. We listen to the rain and feel damp, but the thick canopy formed by the leafy treetops keeps most of the rain from falling to the forest floor. We smell the moist air.

We see colorful mushrooms growing on fallen logs. We hear the buzzing of insects and see a line of leaf-cutter ants marching across the forest floor carrying tiny pieces of leaf. We hear monkeys dropping nuts from the canopy to the floor and can see their forms moving swiftly in the treetops. Most animals are hiding, but we sense they are watching us and wondering what we are doing there in their wondrous world. This is the rainforest, a place with more life than any other on the planet! We opened our eyes feeling peaceful.

From out of the green "treasure chest" I removed a book, *Here is the Tropical Rain Forest* by Madeleine Dunphy (Hyperion, 1994). We loved this beautiful book that pulled us further into the world of the tropical rainforest and the animals that lived there. We talked about how interconnected all the creatures of the forest are—they all needed each other to live. Each planet and animal had a special place or "niche." The children were thrilled to learn that this complicated habitat was home to our new Animals of the Month. They already had learned from our study of monarchs, bears, bats, wolves, and whales how important taking care of their habitat was for their survival. Now we were to study the creatures

## *Did You Know?* RAINFOREST FACTS

○ Almost two-thirds of the fresh water on earth is cycled in tropical rainforests.

○ Every minute an area of rainforest the size of ten city blocks is lost. At that rate, it will be gone by the year 2081.

○ Rainforests cover only 7% of the earth's surface, and yet they are home to about 50% of all lifeforms.

○ The rainforest flower, Rafflesia, is the largest in the world. It is over three feet wide and smells like rotting meat to attract insects.

○ Trees in the rainforest can grow to over 130 feet tall.

○ Twenty-five percent of the medicines we use come from rainforest plants such as the rosy periwinkle. It grows only in the rainforests of Madagascar and is used to treat childhood leukemia and to save many lives.

○ Foods such as bananas, pineapple, and cocoa originated in tropical rainforests.

○ Rainforests are sometimes called "the lungs of the earth." All the giant trees take carbon dioxide out of the air and create the oxygen we need to breathe.

○ Indigenous people have been living in the rainforests for tens of thousands of years.

○ Forty percent of the world's rainforests have already been destroyed.

○ One kind of giant lily pad in the Amazon grows to be five to eight feet across.

○ Rainforest plants called Epiphytes have roots that never touch the ground. They take moisture from the air.

○ There are more species of fish in the Amazon than in the Atlantic Ocean.

of the rainforest and their green home! "Did they have problems?" we wondered. Many were new and strange to us, and we were anxious to start learning more about these animals that were so different from the ones here at home.

## Literature Connections:

The next day, Helen pulled another book out of the green treasure box. It was *The Kapok Tree* by Lynne Cherry (Harcourt Brace Jovanovich, 1990). The author had spent time in the rainforest so she could draw correctly the plants and animals that live in this great green place! As the story was read we attended with careful Earth Listener ears so we could learn more about the rainforest. In the story a man comes into the forest and falls asleep under a great kapok tree. He has come to cut it down, but in his dream rainforest creatures and a native child appeal to him to leave the tree intact. Each gives a different reason why the tree is important. We were so relieved when the man finally left the forest and did not chop the tree down! We decided that as we studied more about this place we would turn our room into a rainforest. The planning began, and we all knew we wanted a great kapok tree! Here's what we did.

### SIX EASY STEPS TO A RAINFOREST ENVIRONMENT

### STEP 1: A Profusion of Parrots

We surrounded ourselves with a variety of fiction and nonfiction books about birdlife in the region. We created brightly colored parrots to hang from the classroom ceiling. We traced cardboard pieces of feathers, a body and a beak, and assembled them into a fantastic flying flock! We learned that many tropical birds are endangered because they are taken out of the rainforest to be sold in the world pet trade. Some like the Oh-oh from the Hawaiian rainforest became extinct long ago, all because people wanted to wear their lovely feathers! We thought that feathers should

82

have been left on the birds! Our room was already beginning to look more like a rainforest. Some drew other birds for display by carefully observing them in our beautiful books. We also watched them quietly on our wonderful fieldtrip to the rainforest in our local zoo. There is much to observe when one is a serious Earthkeeper!

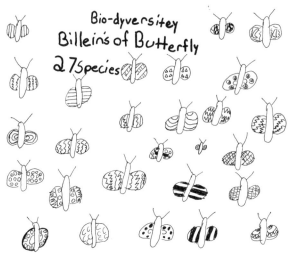

## STEP 2: Billions of Butterflies

We also had a wonderful time studying and creating another abundant creature— the rainforest butterfly. We especially liked the morpho with its iridescent blue wings. Many others have fascinating symmetry and we loved looking at them and designing our own species. We were learning another big but wonderful word — biodiversity. It means many forms of life. The rainforest is full of biodiversity and our room was beginning to be! We placed our butterflies all over the wall above the blackboard and on the windows. The bright copy paper we had cut them out of looked beautiful with the sun coming through it! We played the rainforest tape in the background to inspire us while we created our own rainforest room. We thought it was amazing that there are so many species of butterflies in one place, and scientists think many have not even been discovered yet. We liked the camouflage some developed for protection, like the owl butterfly, which has a spot on each wing that looks like the eye of an owl.

## STEP 3: Teeming Tendrils

We wanted our room to look beautifully "complicated" like the real rainforest so we knew we needed vines. We became vine-producing machines, much like the rainforest! There was many a tongue clinched tightly in teeth as we concentrated on cutting the vines. Marvelous discussions often occurred during these collaborative work sessions as we brainstormed to create the look of a rainforest. We cut our vines from bulletin board paper in shades of green and brown. They looked great in our emerging forest!

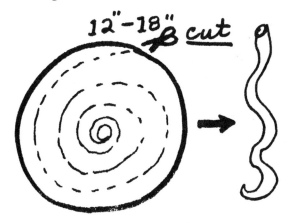

## STEP 4: Beautiful Blossoms

Tissue-paper flowers helped us create the illusion of the vibrant colors of the rainforest with its lush tropical vegetation. This simple circle pattern

led to endless variations as we began to recreate according to our own observations and imagination. Layer two to four circles of tissue that are three to six inches across; pinch at the center. Roll the "stem" in the fingers and secure with a small piece of tape at the base to hold the blossom shape. These can be attached to the vines to achieve a profusion of color.

### STEP 5: Animals
### (Don't Forget the Bugs!)

We read another incredible book, *River* by Judith Gilliland (Clarion, 1993). This told a story of the 4,000-mile journey of the Amazon River through the forests of South America. This and other books helped us learn about the vast variety of animals that call the rainforest home. Wow! Now this is biodiversity! We drew many animals to add to our rainforest bulletin board where we had placed pages from a calendar we really liked, called **Listen to the Children: The Rainforest—Our**

**World, Our Vision** (Visions United, 1993–95). Children from all over the world had drawn their visions of the rainforest. We could tell from the beauty of their art that they loved the rainforest as we did. It's amazing! We are thousands of miles apart but together in the heart! We also painted animals on bulletin board paper, stuffed them with batting, stapled them together, and placed them in our forest. We tried to approximate their real size when we could. We could learn forever about the animals of the rainforest. There are so many!

### STEP 6: The Kapok Tree

We finally dedicated our kapok tree. We had made it by crumpling newspaper and taping it to a volleyball standard until it was the right shape. We covered it with crumpled brown paper and attached empty dead branches to the top of the pole with duct tape. Finally, the teacher attached leaves we had made and draped our tendrils. We thought it looked great. We knew it wasn't like a real kapok tree, but it gave us that tropical feeling. Now we wanted to learn even more about the wonders of the rainforest!

# Integrating the Idea:

## LANGUAGE ARTS:
## Reports on Animals from A-Z!

We divided into partners to work on rainforest animal reports. As we researched we made web charts of the attributes of our animals. We watched Part 1 of *You Can't Grow Home Again*, a fantastic video about life in the rainforest.

## SCIENCE/MATH:
## Layers of Life

We had learned there were four major layers of life in the rainforest: emergents, the

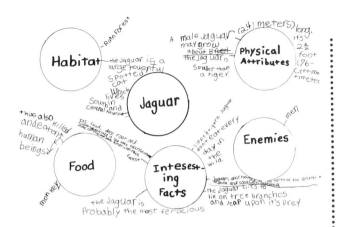

Habitat — Rainforest*
the Jaguar is a large powerful spotted cat
which lives in South and Central America

Jaguar

A male Jaguar may grow about 8 feet the Jaguar is smaller than a tiger

Physical Attributes
(2.4) meters) long, it's 2½ foot (76-centimeter

Food
+has also killed and eaten human beings
monkey

Interesting Facts
It's loud deep roar and
the Jaguar likes to lie on tree branches and leap upon it's prey
the Jaguar is probably the most ferocious

Enemies — men
Lions, tigers, jaguar don't eat every day in the wild.

canopy, the understory, and the forest floor. Different life exists in all these layers. We created a small rainforest bulletin board. (One centimeter equaled two feet.) We made tiny animals and tried to place them in the proper level of our miniature rainforest. We knew our emergent trees (the few that break out and grow above the canopy) can grow to 300 feet tall, which is as long as a football field. However, most grow to be about 150 feet, which is incredible! We illustrated what we had learned about levels and wrote rainforest "facts" we were accumulating. We had a "What I Know About the Rainforest" journal where we could place our information.

## What I know about the rainforest:

It Rains Lats
Tar is a Canopy
Tar is a Sloth
Tar is a Monkey
Tarisa 2Can
Taris a butterfly

## SCIENCE/MATH:
## Measuring a Miracle

We took an adding machine tape and marked off 150 feet, one foot at a time. We taped this to the wall in the hallway. It kept going and going! Most trees in the rainforest are eighty to 150 feet tall. We found out that our school was only twenty-five feet tall.

## SCIENCE/MATH:
## Terrarium Treasures

We were learning that many of our common houseplants originally came from the plants in the rainforests. In fact, two-thirds of the flowering plants in the world came from there. We recycled some two-liter pop bottles. We cut off the top part with the spout on it and pulled off the bottom reinforcer. We put dirt in this section and placed a small species of plant in it that would have originally come from the rainforest. We then turned the rounded bottom part upside down over the plant to create a terrarium. We could watch the transpiration of the moisture in the air and imagined how much water the huge trees of the Amazon could cycle. We also had a big earth terrarium in the class and could really see moisture form!

## SCIENCE/MATH:
## Money Matters

We had been learning from our reading, guest experts, and research about the problems facing the rainforest today. We wanted

to help, so we started to plan a bakesale to be held at school. Each item would cost one quarter. We practiced ways to make change from a dollar so when the sale days came, we would be able to serve our customers well.

## SOCIAL STUDIES: Rainforests Have People

- **A book about a child of the Amazon.** We read *Amazon Boy* by Ted Lewin (Macmillan, 1993). The boy in the story lives in the Amazon rainforest and realizes how special his home is when he visits the city downstream. At the end of the story he makes an important choice! It seems that there are Earthkeepers all over the planet making choices.

- **Reading a folktale.** We read a folktale the Amazon boy might have liked, *Papagayo: The Mischief Maker* by Gerald McDermott (HBJ, 1992). In this vibrantly illustrated story we met Papagayo, a parrot, who reminded us of the "trickster" characters in our Native American unit. Then we realized that the natives of the rainforest were also Native Americans. They had lived in the rainforests of South America for thousands of years! We loved this tale of a moon-dog who is eating the moon a little bit more every night. Our teacher told us there were many legends about the moon in South American rainforest stories. It was sort of magic!

- **A tale of rubber tappers.** A guest had visited the rainforest and brought back many wonderful items. She showed us animals made from natural rubber. Rubber is made from the liquid latex of rubber trees. Rubber can now be made in other ways but the rubber trees in the rainforest are still very important to protect and use wisely, she said. She showed us a book, *Antonio's Rain Forest* by Anna Lewington (Carolrhoda, 1993). It tells of the life of a boy, Antonio José. His father is a rubber tapper. It explains the history of rubber and the problems rubber tappers face today. It was interesting hearing about real people of the forest!

- **Rainforest schools.** I had visited schools in the Amazon rainforest of Peru and showed pictures of the children. I explained how we could help support a school in the rainforest and write to the children, but we would have the help of someone who speaks Spanish, as that is the language studied in their schools. I told how children there love to play soccer although they only had one ball for the whole school, which was a one-room building with very few supplies. Pencils, paper, and books were treasures to these students. They were very beautiful

people. I wished we could all meet them someday! We looked at our map again to find Peru and the South American rainforest near the equator.

- **Rainforest information center.** We had a center with artifacts from indigenous peoples of the rainforest. We loved the reed flute. Indians respected the forest and knew many of its secrets for their own survival and enjoyment! We watched more of the video *You Can't Grow Home Again* and we didn't like what was happening to the rainforest we were beginning to care so much about! It was being burned and cut down and not carefully respected! We began to think and write about this. We wanted to help this 7% of the planet!

# Celebrations:
## A Bakesale Bonanza

We learned Jim Valley's song "Rainforest" and sang it all the time! In the song he asks, "A diamond ring or a living thing—which has more worth?" We were sure we knew the answer! We sang as we worked. We were Earthkeepers in action!

- **Bookmarks for sale.** We created bookmarks that carried our messages about the rainforest and other areas we had studied. We had them laminated. We were careful not to waste paper as we worked.

- **Parent and school notes.** We designed and sent notes asking parents to donate cookies or fruits for our bakesale. We were going to raise money to protect some rainforest acres. We needed $25 for an acre. We knew if we sponsored the acre it would be protected. It could never be chopped down, burned, or ruined. We made signs to advertise our sale and invited all other classes to come help save the rainforest! We all were going to take

turns running the sale. We had fourth-grade partners who helped us. We did great! We earned enough money to protect twenty-two acres, with the help of everyone in school! They even wrote about us in the newspaper. We were glad to be Earthkeepers sharing an important message! We had explained to all our sale customers why the rainforests were important. We gave them fact fliers to spread the word.

# World Wondering:
## Writing to the President

- **Visualizing an acre.** After we completed our bakesale project we were so happy we celebrated! We walked to a nearby football field to help us visualize our accomplishment. We knew a football field was about one acre and we had adopted twenty-two acres! What we had done really mattered. We stayed there a minute and read *Stop That Noise*, a delightful and thoughtful tale about rainforest destruction by Paul Geraghty (Crown, 1992).

- **A video to celebrate.** We went back to our classroom celebrating! We sipped fruit punch, ate some rainforest crunch, had scoops of Ben and Jerry's Rainforest ice cream, and watched a video, *The Nature Connection*, about Canadian children who had adopted a cloud forest (another type of rainforest). We knew there were different types of rainforests in Africa, Asia, South America, and Australia. Helen said we would learn more later about a great rainforest in our own American Northwest. It was not a tropical rainforest, but it was wonderful, and also was threatened. We were curious to learn about that great forest too! But for now we were in the tropics, and names like Brazil and Peru now held real meaning for us. They are special places on our planet!

February 19, 1993

Dear Mr President,
    My name is Lauren L.
and I am in First Grade at
Metcalf School. We are
studying the Rainforests.
I want to save the
Rainforest! Please tell
me what I can do to
help save the earth! Your
Earth-Keeper friend,
Lauren Lackovich.

- **Book about an Earthkeeper.** The next day we read *Save My Rainforest* by Monica Zak (Volcano Press, 1992) and were glad there were children in the world like the boy in the story who helped save a bit of the rainforests of Mexico! He had written many letters. We decided we would, too. We wrote to the President of the United States telling him how we loved the rainforests. We were glad he wrote back!

# Family Tie:
## A Rainforest Products Search

Our families had been sharing our excitement as we learned about the rainforest! We took home a "Rainforest Product Search" sheet. We were to look for products we had in our homes that originated in the rainforests. We knew that many plants once grown only in the rainforest were now cultivated in greenhouses, but they still owed their lives to their rainforest origins. It was fun searching at home together for products of the rainforest that had become part of our everyday life! We each brought a product to display in our rainforest center. We were celebrating a great new awareness of these treasurehouses of the planet—the tropical rainforests! When we sat down and shared *Welcome to the Greenhouse* by Jane Yolen (Putnam, 1993) we knew we had learned much about this glorious place on the planet! We again remembered our Earthkeeper promise to be curious all our lives. Someday we might help find more ways to use the rainforest without destroying it.

Spring was now near at hand. Millions of migratory birds would soon leave their winter homes in the rainforest and fly north for the summer. They need both habitats to survive. Fortunately for these feathered friends, we are growing-up to be thoughtful Earthkeepers. We care for the whole beautiful planet.

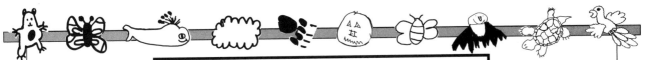

# RAINFOREST PRODUCT SEARCH

**FRUITS AND VEGETABLES**

____ avocado

____ banana

____ grapefruit

____ heart of the palm

____ lemon

____ lime

____ mango

____ orange

____ papaya

____ passion fruit

____ pepper

____ pineapple

____ sweet potato

**HOUSEPLANTS**

____ African violets

____ philodendron

____ Begonia

____ bird's-nest fern

____ bromeliads

____ Christmas cactus

____ Dieffenbachia

____ fiddle-leaf fig

**OILS**

____ banana oil

____ bay

____ camphor

____ coconut oil

____ lime

____ palm oil

**RUBBER PRODUCTS**

____ rubber gloves

____ rubber bands

**SPICES AND FLAVORS**

____ allspice

____ black pepper

____ cayenne

____ chili pepper

____ chocolate or cocoa

____ cinnamon

____ cloves

____ ginger

____ nutmeg

____ paprika

____ turmeric

____ vanilla

**OTHER FOODS**

____ Brazil nuts

____ cashew nuts

____ chewing gum (made from chicle)

____ coffee

____ macadamia nuts

____ tapioca

____ tea

**WOODS**

____ balsa

____ Brazil wood

____ mahogany

____ rosewood

____ sandalwood

____ teak

**CANES AND FIBERS**

____ bamboo

____ kapok

____ rattan

# Books about the Rainforest

**Baker, Jeannie.** *Where the Forest Meets the Sea.* Greenwillow, 1987.

**Cherry, Lynne.** *The Great Kapok Tree.* Harcourt Brace Jovanovich, Orlando, 1990.

**Dunphy, Madeleine.** *Here Is the Tropical Rain Forest.* Hyperion, New York, 1994.

**Fischetto, Laura.** *The Jungle Is My Home.* Viking, New York, 1991.

**Geraghty, Paul.** *Stop That Noise.* Crown, New York, 1992.

**Gibbons, Gail.** *Nature's Green Umbrella: Tropical Rain Forests.* Morrow Junior, New York, 1994.

**Gilliland, Judith Heide.** *River.* Clarion, New York, 1993.

**Jeunesse, Gallimard,** and **Rene Mettler.** *The Rain Forest: A First Discovery Book.* Scholastic, New York, 1992.

**Jordan, Martin,** and **Tanis.** *Journey of the Red-Eyed Tree Frog.* Simon and Schuster, New York, 1991.

**Krulik, Nancy,** and **Phoebe Yeh.** *Save the Rainforest.* Scholastic, New York, 1992.

**Lewin, Ted.** *Amazon Boy.* Macmillan, New York, 1993.

**Morris, Joshua.** *Rainforest: Nature Search.* Reader's Digest, Pleasantville, New York, 1992.

**Nayer, Judy.** *Come On into the Rain Forest.* Modern Curriculum, Cleveland, 1993.

**Pratt, Kristin.** *A Walk in the Rainforest.* Dawn, Nevada, 1992.

**Uchitel, Sandra.** *Endangered Animals of the Rainforest.* Price Stern Sloan, Los Angeles, 1992.

**Yolen, Jane.** *Welcome to the Greenhouse: A Story of the Tropical Rainforest.* Putnam, New York, 1993.

**Zak, Monica.** *Save My Rainforest.* Volcano Press, Volcano, California, 1992.

## AUDIOVISUAL MATERIALS

*Jim Valley: Friends Around the World* (Cassette). Rainbow Planet Records, 5110 Cromwell Drive, Gig Harbor, WA 98335., 1993

*You Can't Grow Home Again* (VHS). Children's Television Workshop, Box HV, One Lincoln Plaza, New York, NY 10023.

## REFERENCES

**Chinery, Michael.** *Rainforest Animals.* Random House, New York, 1992.

**Ganeri, Anita.** *Explore the World of Exotic Rainforests.* Western, Wisconsin,1992.

**Goodman, Billy.** *Planet Earth: The Rain Forest.* Little, New York, 1992.

**Silver, Donald.** *Why Save the Rainforest?* Julian Messner, New York, 1993.

**Taylor, Barbara.** *Look Closer: Rain Forest.* Dorling Kindersley, New York, 1992.

## NOTES:

To inquire about the Protect-An-Acre Program, contact The Nature Conservancy, 1815 M. Lynn St., Arlington, Virginia 22209, 1-800-628-6860 or Rainforest Action Network, 450 Sansome, Suite 700, San Francisco, California 94111. (There are other acre adoption programs through great organizations such as World Wildlife Fund. Check it out and make sure other groups are reliable.

To support a rainforest school, contact International Expeditions, 801 Deven Place, Alexandria, Virginia 22314, 1-800-669-6806.

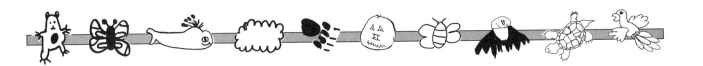

# The Coming of Spring

*"The last fling of winter is over....*
*The earth, the soil itself has a dreaming quality about it.*
*It is warm now to the touch; it has come alive;*
*it hides secrets that in a moment,*
*in a little while, it will tell."*

— Donald Culross Peattie

Once again the wonder of the season slipped up on us! The feel of spring is all around, and anticipation is in the air. When will we see the first bud? When will we see the first robin? When will we see the first crocus push its head through the thawing earth? None of us knows for certain, and that is part of the magic. We have come to love the waiting and the looking!

**A List of Firsts:** It wasn't long ago that we were looking for the first snowflakes. Now we are searching for the first flowers. We begin our "Signs of Spring Observation Journal" and soon it is blossoming along with the awakening earth. This will be a busy season for Earthkeepers. Many activities are in store as we observe, document, and celebrate this season.

with a tiny begonia that he/she could take home and plant. We raised our hands and pledged "I promise to plant the planet and always be curious about the earth. We knew planting green things was one way we could help!

## Earth Minute:

### "Going Green"

When St. Patrick's Day came we celebrated our Earthkeeper ethic by making "Going Green" buttons. We were thinking a lot about things we could do for the earth.

### Plant the Planet

One Earth Minute I presented each child

## To Hatch a Chick!

We were excited to be hatching chicks and ducks right in our classroom. We were to learn much about those wonderful life cycles in the springtime patterns of the planet! We had to be extremely patient and careful Earthkeepers as we tended and turned the eggs. We were about to witness miracles.

## A Time for Trees

The earth's energy level seems to be bursting forth into high gear and so is ours. Our curiosity is on alert for wonders to behold so we spring deeper into spring! The trees are beginning to leaf out and we turn our attention to them. We remember the leaves we had studied in the fall and now we saw new ones coming!

- **Artist returns.** Our artist friend returned so we could draw our spring and summer trees. Now we had all four seasons of the Earth!

- **Tree sap wonders.** We read *When Spring Comes* by Natalie Kinsey Warnock and thought about maple syrup, which is surely one of the sweetest wonders of trees.

- **Pancake treat.** We learned how maple syrup is produced then celebrated with a pancake breakfast using real maple syrup from Vermont. It was delicious!

- **Celebrating Arbor Day.** We planned to plant a tree on Arbor Day and learn more about why this holiday is celebrated. We knew trees provided us with many products from food to pure enjoyment. We learned about and listed these products and pleasures.

- **Paper is a gift of trees.** One day a special Earthkeeper, Mrs. Perez, showed us how to make paper. It was great fun listening to her as she talked about this gift of the trees. She wrote a book called *Explore and Experiment* (First Teacher, 1988) which tells how she makes paper! Paper is a great gift, but now that we knew where it came from, we would be careful not to waste it. An Earthkeeper is never careless with a gift of nature!

- **Trouble in the forest.** We learned that many of the earth's forests are being cut down. We know we need the wood from trees, but we also hoped a way could be found to protect some of the old forests that have been home for creatures of the planet for thousands of years! We are Earthkeepers and perhaps we will help find solutions someday, but for now we can plant trees and learn about them and love them. We learned a poem by Margaret Mahy called "The Pines." It told the story of great pine trees being cut down. Some of the words are, "Seventy years have made them tall. It takes ten minutes to make them fall!" We read another book called *10 Tall Oaktrees* by Richard Edwards (Tambourine, 1988). In the story people cut down all the trees in the grove over the years. One day, however, a young boy comes along and finds an acorn from the last tree. He carefully plants it and sprouts a baby tree. We can all be that boy (or that girl)! We watched a video called *The Man Who Loved Trees*, and we decided Giorno, the man in the story, was certainly an Earth Hero! He loved trees like we do!

- **History told in trees.** Trees hold many incredible secrets, some of which are only learned after the tree is dead. We learned about the rings inside the trunk of the trees. These layers, or growth rings, tell the tree's age—another amazing circle of

nature! We had a cross section of tree to look at on the story stump, and we tried to count the rings. There were so many. Our friend was very old!

- **A personal tree tale.** We decided to draw a tree cross section that would represent our lives. We labeled the rings according to events in our lives. Finally, we wrote a story on the theme, "My Best Time on Earth!"

> My Best Time on the earth was
> win i was three and i cod read.

> SPring is a happy time.
> That I love. It is fun.
> you see animals evey were.
> and you see flowers.
> I love flowers. don't you.
> don't you love sPring.
> I do. We go fishing.
> and see basas.
> I like basas. do you
>    I love evey thing

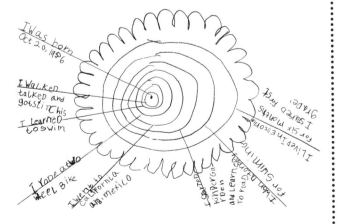

Jenna had noticed that the frogs were beginning to croak again—a sure sign of spring and of a healthy planet! We did reports on frogs and toads and then celebrated by writing our own songs to the joy of spring! The cycles of the earth are in a time of great promise and we will always remember this spring! We read *Little Frog's Song* by Alice Schertle (HarperCollins, 1992) and were happy with the choice made by the young Earthkeeper in the story!

# Books about Spring

**Alexander, Sue.** *There's More...Much More.* Harcourt Brace Jovanovich, New York, 1991.

**Ardley, Neil.** *The Science Book of Things That Grow.* Harcourt Brace Jovanovich, New York, 1991.

**Atkinson, Allen.** *Jack in the Green.* Crown, New York, 1987.

**Demi.** *Demi's Secret Garden.* Henry Holt, New York, 1993.

**Emberley, Ed.** *Three Science Flip Books.* Little, Brown, New York, 1982.

**Herriot, James.** *Smudge, The Little Lost Lamb.* St. Martin's, New York, 1991.

**Hirschi, Ron.** *Spring.* Cobblehill, New York, 1990.

**Kelly, M. A.** *A Child's Book of Wildflowers.* Four Winds, New York, 1992.

**Kinsey-Warnock, Natalie.** *When Spring Comes.* Dutton, New York, 1993.

**Krauss, Ruth.** *The Happy Day.* Harper & Row, New York, 1949.

**Pfister, Marcus.** *Hopper Hunts for Spring.* North-South, New York, 1992.

**Rockwell, Anne.** *My Spring Robin.* Macmillan, New York, 1989.

**Schweninger, Ann.** *Let's Look at the Seasons: Springtime.* Viking, New York, 1993.

**Skofield, James.** *Crow Moon, Worm Moon.* Macmillan, New York, 1990.

**Vyner, Sue.** *Arctic Spring.* Viking, New York, 1993.

**Wilkes, Angels.** *My First Garden Book.* Alfred A. Knopf, New York, 1992.

## BOOKS ABOUT THE EGG

**Barber, Antonia.** *Gemma and the Baby Chick.* Scholastic, New York, 1992.

**Burton, Robert.** *Egg: A Photographic Story of Hatching.* Dorling Kindersley, New York, 1994.

**Heller, Ruth.** *Chickens Aren't the Only Ones.* Scholastic, New York, 1981.

**Jeunesse, Gallimard.** *The Egg.* Scholastic, New York, 1989.

**Polacco, Patricia.** *Rechenka's Eggs.* Philomel, New York, 1988.

## BOOKS ABOUT FROGS

**Gibbons, Gail.** *Frogs.* Holiday House, New York, 1993.

**Hirschi, Ron.** *Hungry Little Frog.* Cobblehill (Dutton), New York, 1992.

**Kindersley, Dorling.** *See How They Grow: Frog.* Lodestar (Dutton), New York, 1991.

**Schertle, Alice.** *Little Frog's Song.* HarperCollins, New York, 1992.

**Snape, Juliet,** and **Charles.** *Frog Odyssey.* Simon and Schuster, New York, 1992.

**Welber, Robert.** *Frog Frog Frog.* Pantheon, New York, 1971.

## BOOKS ABOUT TREES AND ARBOR DAY

**Anholt, Laurence.** *The Forgotten Forest.* Sierra Club, San Francisco, 1992.

**Appelbaum, Diana.** *Giants in the Land.* Houghton Mifflin, Boston, 1993.

**Arnosky, Jim.** *I was Born in a Tree and Raised by Bees.* Bradbury, New York, 1977.

**Ayres, Pam.** *When Dad Cuts Down the Chestnut Tree.* Walker, Pleasant Hill, 1988.

**Bash, Barbara.** *Ancient Ones: The World of the Old Growth Douglas Fir.* Sierra Club Books, San Francisco, 1994.

**Bash, Barbara.** *Tree of Life: The Word of the African Baobab.* Little, Brown, Boston, 1989.

**Behn, Harry.** *Trees.* Henry Holt, New York, 1992.

**Bellamy, David.** *The Forest: Our Changing World.* Clarkson N. Potter, New York, 1988.

**Brenner, Barbara.** *The Tremendous Tree Book.* Scholastic, New York, 1979.

**Bunting, Eve.** *Someday a Tree.* Clarion, New York, 1993.

**Burns, Diane L.** *Arbor Day.* Carolrhoda, Minneapolis, 1989.

**Edwards, Richard.** *Ten Tall Oaktrees.* Tambourine, New York, 1993.

**Gackenbach, Dick.** *Mighty Tree.* Harcourt Brace Jovanovich, New York, 1992.

**Gibbons, Gail.** *Frogs.* Holiday House, New York, 1993.

**Gile, John.** *The First Forest.* Worzalla, Stevens Point, Wisconsin, 1989.

**Haseley, Dennis.** *My Father Doesn't Know About the Woods and Me.* Antheneum New York, 1988.

**Hirschi, Ron.** *Forest.* Bantam, New York, 1991.

**Ikeda, Daisaku.** *The Cherry Tree.* Alfred A. Knopf, New York, 1991.

**Kalman, Bobbie,** and **Janine Schaub.** *How Trees Help Me.* Crabtree, New York, 1992.

**Lauber, Patricia.** *Be a Friend to Trees.* HarperCollins, New York, 1994.

**Lavies, Bianca.** *Tree Trunk Traffic.* E. P. Dutton, New York, 1989.

**Levine, Arthur.** *Pearl Moscowitz's Last Stand.* Tambourine, New York, 1993.

**Lionni, Leo.** *A Busy Year.* Alfred A. Knopf, New York, 1992.

**Lottridge, Celia Barker.** *The Name of the Tree: A Bantu Folktale Retold.* Macmillan, New York, 1989.

**Luenn, Nancy.** *Song for the Ancient Forest.* Atheneum, New York, 1993.

**Lyon, George Ella.** *ABCEDAR: An Alphabet of Trees.* Orchard, New York, 1989.

**Manson, Christopher.** *The Tree in The Wood: An Old Nursery Song.* North-South, New York, 1993.

**Peet, Bill.** *Farewell to Shady Glade.* Houghton Mifflin, Boston, 1966.

**Quinn, Greg Henry.** *A Gift of a Tree.* Scholastic New York, 1994.

**Romanova, Natalia.** *Once There Was a Tree.* Dial, New York, 1985.

**Ryder, Joanne.** *Hello, Tree!.* Dutton, New York, 1991.

**Thornhill, Jan.** *A Tree in a Forest.* Simon & Schuster, New York, 1991.

**Tresselt, Alvin.** *The Gift of the Tree.* Lothrop, Lee & Shepard, New York, 1992.

**Wirth, Victoria.** *Whisper from the Woods.* Simon & Schuster, New York, 1991.

## AUDIOVISUAL MATERIALS

*Forests Are More Than Trees.* an Educational Slide/Tape Presentation of the National Wildlife Federation. 1412 Sixteenth Street, NW, Washington, D.C. 20036-2266.

*In Celebration of Trees: The World's Oldest Living Things* (VHS). A discovery Channel Production, Discovery Program Enterprises, Bethseda, Maryland 20814

*The Man Who Planted Trees* (VHS).Direct Cinema Ltd., P. O. Box 10003, Santa Monica, California 90410.

## BOOKS ABOUT "GOING GREEN"

**Bellamy, David.** *How Green Are You?.* Clarkson Potter, New York, 1991.

**Brown, Paurie Krasny,** and **Marc Brown.** *Dinosaurs to the Rescue!: A Guide to Protecting Our Planet.* Little, Brown, Boston, 1992.

**Wilkes, Angela.** *My First Green Book.* Alfred A. Knopf, New York, 1991.

# The Wonder of Land

*"This land is your land, this land is my land.*
*This land was made for you and me!"*

—Woody Guthrie

Latent in almost all of us, there is a strong connection to the soil of the planet. Watch children as they play in the mud after a spring rain or note their fascination while digging in a garden or building elaborate sand castles at a beach. Children not only love the planet, they also love the soil! Rocks are a never-ending source of intrigue. We have celebrated water and air and now we honor the land itself as did the Native Americans.

## Earth Minute:
### Everybody Needs a Rock

I called the children to the story stump once again and shared the book *Everybody Needs A Rock* by Byrd Baylor (Scribners, 1974). It is a wonderful story that lays down ten rules to consider when selecting a rock. At the end of the story each child chose one very special rock to keep from a basket of

rocks. The Earth Center was stocked with rocks for sorting and classifying. During the land study we learned about the effects water and air can have on the land through erosion. We also learned reasons the soil is important to us all and why we should take care not to pollute it or let it blow and wash away!

## A Planet Caretaker:
### Miss Rumphius

- **A tale about the power of plants.** One of the most important uses of soil is for growing plants for food, air, and beauty.

*I name My Rock Softie*

## Did You Know?
## LAND FACTS

○ The earth is four and one half billion years old. The land is always changing shape. Some scientists believe that millions of years ago all the continents were connected.

○ People have changed the land a great deal by cutting down whole forests and building farms and cities.

○ The highest point of land on earth is Mt. Everest at 29,028 feet.

○ The earth is not perfectly round. It is slightly flat at the North Pole and bulges out at the equator.

○ Some of the world's tallest mountains are under the ocean.

○ Soil is composed primarily of dead plant matter.

○ We throw away enough glass bottles and jars to fill the 13,500-foot Twin Towers of New York's World Trade Center every two weeks.

○ Every year Americans receive about two million tons of junk mail. Forty-four percent of this is never even opened!

○ American consumers and industry throw away enough aluminum to rebuild our entire commercial airfleet every three months.

This is a tale of a young girl who grows up and travels the globe, but knows that to fulfill her grandfather's words she must find something beautiful to do for the world. When she herself is an elderly woman, she plants lupine seeds and begins a beautiful transformation of the landscape.

This cycle of growth took a long time but was worth the wait. We thought about what we each might do to make the planet a more beautiful place.

## Saving Energy:
### Guest Experts

● **Seeing solar power.** As we looked more closely at the wonderful resources of the land, our special guests Rick and John returned to talk about energy.

Rick took a small glass object out of a box. It had a little wheel on the top of the rod. There were black-and-white plates attached. When Rick sat it in the sun it began to turn. Rick explained that this was powered by the sun. We were witnessing the power of solar energy!

● **Energy transfer.** Rick and John also showed us how the energy from the sun is trapped in the foods we eat and transferred to us when we consume them—an amazing earth circle!

Rick poured some cornflakes from a box and ate them, while John talked about the history of the cornflakes before they were put into the box. The corn seed had been placed in the soil. It was rained on by the earth's water and then pushed up through the soil and emerged into the light of the sun. The sun's energy was absorbed by the growing corn plant and it grew like crazy!

All of a sudden, bursting with energy, Rick jumped up and ran over to the piano and began to play. He had been filled with energy from the earth, he said!

● **Other energy forms.** We learned about wind and water energy, too. We talked about how solar and wind energy were cleaner than the energy Rick had showed us a few months ago when he started a car outside our classroom.

We remembered how dirty the cloth became when it was placed over the exhaust pipe. We saw that good Earthkeepers will need to study sources of energy to be able to make wise choices for the needs of people and the earth.

# Earth Minute:

## Earth in the Dumpster

The children came into the room one day and saw a small wading pool full of bottles, cans, and paper. In the middle of it all I had placed a globe. "Is this any way to take care of the Earth?" a sign asked. They were fascinated and during the following Earth Minute we discussed garbage. Where does it come from? What's in it? Where does it go? How does it affect the earth? We decided we wanted to learn more about it. We broke into small groups and each group wrote a short story on "The History of Garbage." This was fun, but we also realized there was a lot we didn't know about trash.

- **A garbage video.** The next day we watched *The Dirty Rotten Truth About Garbage*. It was great! We learned that when we throw resources away we are wasting the earth's energy! The trash on our curb goes to a place called a landfill and is buried or burned. What a waste. We already knew a lot about recycling and reusing our resources but we wanted to learn even more. We planned a double fieldtrip.

- **Field trip to a Recycle Center.** First we visited a recycling center. We saw mountains of paper that were being recycled! Yeah! We saw bottles being smashed to be reused and aluminum cans crushed. We saw resources and energy being saved! We liked this. Then we went to visit a landfill.

- **Field trip to a landfill.** It was huge—a gigantic garbage sandwich! Seeing is worth a thousand words, and we could "see" energy wasted everywhere we looked. "Why are they doing this?" Joseph asked as he looked on in disbelief. "I'm glad I don't waste stuff," he continued.

- **Processing our thoughts.** We went back to school and discussed the trip. Wasting a piece of paper would never be the same! We decided to share what we had seen.

- **Trash or treasure display case.** We helped put together two display cases to show the choices we all can make. We can choose to have a beautiful Earth on which to live or we can trash it up with junk that makes the Earth ugly and wastes its resources. Her resources are all the things we need to live, so it isn't very smart to waste them!

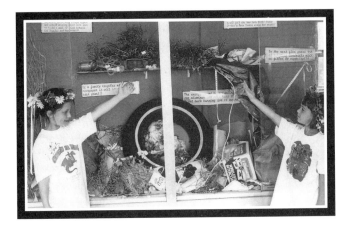

- **Earth chants.** We wrote chants and started Earth Journals about ways we are learning to help the earth.

- **Landfill bulletin board.** We drew pictures to illustrate our landfill visions and displayed them in the hallway. The landfill reminded us of *Wump World* by Bill Peet (Houghton Mifflin, 1970). We are really messing up our planet! And the recycling center made us think about *The Lorax* by Dr. Seuss (Random House, 1971) and all the truffula trees. This was not paper waste from a truffula tree but from real trees on a real earth. It was good to recycle it and not just throw it away!

- **Alternatives centers.** We set up a center where we could display "alternatives'" to wasteful practices. We had string, shopping bags, and reusable lunch boxes among other items!

- **Visualizing waste.** We tried to think up ways to show how many resources we were wasting. We made a pile of newspaper 31 inches high and made a sign that read, "This equals one tree."

- **Teaching our parents.** We shared what we were learning with our families. We

were always going to practice the 3 Rs!
No wasting the Earth for us!

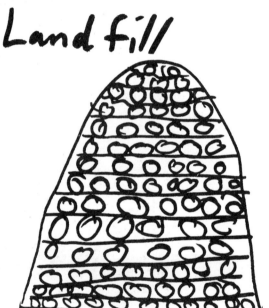

## The Three Rs:
## Reduce, Recycle, Reuse

(An Earth song to the Planet's Children)
by Dee and Hans Damkoehler

We have really got a problem
But there are things that you can do.
All you kids can start conserving—
That means saving things we use.

Save your aluminum, your plastic, and
    your glass;
Save all the paper that you throw away in
    class.

*Let's all Reduce, Recycle, and Reuse.*
*Oh yeah, the 3 Rs are good for me and you.*
*Oh, I see a brighter day*
*'Cause we're learning a new way.*
*Let's all Reduce, Recycle, and Reuse.*

Let's stop filling up the landfills
And wasting energy.
I feel good now,
'Cause you kids are takin' better care of me.
You can help teach your parents
There is a better way.
I hear a rising chorus as the kids stand up
    and say—

(Everybody stand)

*Let's all Reduce, Recycle, and Reuse.*
*Oh yeah, the 3 Rs are good for me and you.*
*Think about what you use;*
*What you throw away you lose.*
*Let's all Reduce, Recycle, and Reuse.*

—from the Illimois ENR Video *Reduce,*
*Reuse, Recycle: It's Elementary*
(217) 785-2800

searched for the items we had placed in our boot soup we discovered an interesting pattern. The leaves, banana peel, bark, etc. were gone or almost gone. The plastic cherries, six pack rings, glass jar, aluminum can, etc. were still in good shape. Mark observed, "It looks like if the Earth made it she will take it back, but if people made it she won't!" We talked about the need to help the Earth take back the things she can't on her own. People can help by recycling!

See p. 28

# Return to the Old Boot:

## An Adventure in Compost

When we opened up our old boot compost aquarium, we were amazed to see a lot of beautiful black dirt had been created as many of the leaves had decomposed and gone back to the earth—in fact, they had become earth! It was so black, and it didn't smell bad at all. Parts of our old boot were still there, but a lot of it had gone back to the earth. As we

# Books about Land

**Arnosky, Jim.** *Crinkleroot's Guide to Walking in Wild Places.* Bradbury, New York, 1990.

**Baker, Jeanine.** *Window.* Greenwillow, New York, 1991.

**Bellamy, David.** *The Roadside.* Clarkson and Potter, New York, 1988.

**Bliss, Corinne.** *Matthew's Meadow.* Harcourt Brace Jovanovich, San Diego, 1992.

**Gerson, Mary-Joan.** *Why the Sky Is Far Away: A Nigerian Folktale.* Little Brown, Boston, 1992.

**Hiscock, Bruce.** *The Big Rock.* Antheneum, New York, 1988.

**MacDonald, Golden and Leonard Wisegard.** *The Little Island.* Doubleday, New York, 1946.

**Miller, Edna.** *Mousekin's Lost Woodland.* Simon and Schuster, New York, 1992.

**Myers, Christopher.** *McCrephy's Field.* Houghton Mifflin, Boston, 1991.

**Parnell, Peter.** *The Rock.* Macmillan, New York, 1991.

**Peet, Bill.** *The Wump World.* Houghton Mifflin, Boston, 1970.

**San Souci, Daniel.** *Country Road.* Doubleday, New York, 1993.

**Schmid, Eleonore.** *The Living Earth.* North-South, New York, 1994.

**Stille, Darlene.** *Soil Erosion and Pollution.* Children's Press, Chicago, 1990.

**Symes, R. F.** *Rocks and Minerals.* Alfred A. Knopf, New York, 1988.

**Thiele, Colin.** *Farmer Schulz's Ducks.* Harper, New York, 1988.

**Turner, Anne.** *Heron Street.* Harper and Row, New York, 1989.

**Wheeler, Jill.** *The Land We Live On.* Abdo and Daughters, Edina, Minnesota, 1990.

**Wildsmith, Brian,** and **Rebecca.** *Jack and the Meanstalk.* Knopf, New York, 1994.

## AUDIOVISUAL MATERIALS

*Soil: We Can't Grow Without It.* Slide/Tape Presentation of the National Wildlife Federation, 412 Sixteenth Street NW, Washington, D. C. 20036.

# Books about Solid Waste/Recycling

**Berenstain, Stan and Jan.** *Don't Pollute (Anymore)*. Random House, New York, 1991.

**Brown, Laurie Kransny.** *Dinosaurs to the Rescue!* Little, Brown, Boston, 1992.

**Gibbons, Gail.** *Recycle: A Handbook for Kids.* Little, Brown, Boston, 1992.

**Glimmerveen, Ulco.** *A Tale of Antarctica.* Scholastic, New York, 1990.

**Leedy, Loreen.** *The Great Trash Bash.* Holiday House, New York, 1991.

**Madden, Don.** *The Wartville Wizard.* Aladdin Books, New York, 1993.

**Newton-John, Olivia.** *A Pig Tale.* Simon and Schuster, New York, 1993.

**Showers, Paul.** *Where Does the Garbage Go?.* HarperCollins, New York, 1994.

**The Earth Works Group.** *50 Simple Things Kids Can Do To Recycle.* EarthWorks Press, Berkeley, California, 1994.

**Williams, Karen Lynn.** *Galimoto*. Lothrop, New York, 1990

## AUDIOVISUAL MATERIALS

*Earth to Kids* (VHS). Video, Inc., 5547 North Ravenswood Avenue, Chicago, IL 60640-1199.

*The Rotten Truth* (VHS). Children's Television Workshop, Box HV, One Limcoln Plaza, New York, NY 10023.

## REFERENCES

**Fleming, Maria.** *Garbage: Theme Unit Based on Activities from the Hackensack Meadowlands Development Commission Environment Center.* Scholastic, New York, 1991.

**Foster, Joanna.** *Carton, Cans, and Orange Peels: Where Does Your Garbage Go?.* Clarion, New York, 1991.

**Kalbacken, Joan,** and **Emilie U. Lepthien.** *Recycling.* Children's Press, Chicago, 1991.

**Kallen, Stuart A.** *Recycle It. Once Is Not Enough!* Abdo and Daughters, Edina, Minnesota, 1990.

**Kalman, Bobbie.** *Reducing, Reusing, and Recycling.* Crabtree, New York, 1991.

**McHarry, Jan.** *The Great Recycling Adventure.* Turner Publishing, Atlanta, 1994.

**Van Allsburg, Chris.** *Just A Dream.* Houghton Mifflin, Boston, 1990.

**Wilcox, Charlotte.** *Trash!* Carolrhoda, Minneapolis, 1988.

# Back Home
# On the Prairie

*"...the secret of wisdom is to be curious—*
*to take time to look closely,*
*to use all your senses to see and touch*
*and taste and smell and hear.*
*To keep on wandering and wondering."*
—From *The Wise Woman and her Secret* by Eve Merriam

## A Time of Celebration:

We began our year on the prairie of our Illinois home. We've traveled far, and now, as the year comes full circle, we return home. It is a time for celebration.

- **Making earth shirts.** We made Earth Shirts as we celebrated our year becoming Earthkeepers! In the blues and greens of the earth, we painted our hands, because we knew we really did have our hands on the planet! We loved all the things we had come to know! We cared about the earth!

- **Reading about Rachel Carson.** We read a rookie biography about a very important Earthkeeper, Rachel Carson. She was a friend of nature and wrote books that helped people understand how our actions affect the planet.

- **An Earthkeeper's counting book.** We read *3 Pandas Planting* by Meghan Halsey (Bradbury, 1994). This is a

counting book full of activities to help us save the earth. We liked it so much we illustrated our own versions.

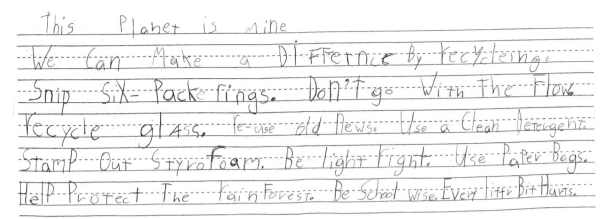

This Planet is Mine

We Can Make a DiFFerrnce By recycleing.
Snip Six-Packe rings. Don't go With The Flow.
recycle glass. re-use old News. Use a Clean Detergent.
Stamp Out StyroFoam. Be light right. Use Paper Bags.
Help Protect The rainForest. Be School wise. Every littir Bit Hurts.

- **Earth journals.** We had begun our Earth Journals earlier and now we wrote in them every day adding a new "Earth-Friendly" idea.

Recide
Save
The Earth

I can make a difference
By Rideing the Bike.
I can Make a difference
By siping six-pack rings.
I can Make a difference
By Recikting. Dana

- **The web of life.** We read a story from *The Big Book of our Planet* called *The Earth Game* by Pam Conrad (Dutton, 1993). She tells a tale of children playing with a ball of string in a meadow. They sit in a circle and toss the ball to one another, eventually creating a web of string that connects them all. They take turns acknowledging a single act such as, "A dolphin is freed from a net." With each statement a player tugs on the web. Everyone in the circle can feel the tug. We see that each action one person takes matters to us all. We played the web game ourselves remembering much we had learned over the past year!

We all live in The same web of life

- **Creating a rose garden.** We read *Wanda's Roses* by Pat Brisson (Boyds Mills Press, 1994). Wanda discovers what she thinks is a rosebush growing in a trash-filled empty lot. She is determined

**105**

her dead twig is a rose about to bloom. She cleans up the lot while tending to the stick. Because of her faith and determination, the ugly empty lot is finally changed into a lovely rose garden. We liked this transformation and decided to start a rose garden at our school, planting one new rose bush each year. Over the years, we too would be able to see our garden grow as we became older and even wiser Earthkeepers!

- **Earth alphabet books.** We each made a personal alphabet book adding entries based on what we had learned about the Earth.

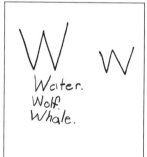

- **Earth Day celebration.** We prepared songs, signs, and chants to perform in our School Earth Day Assembly. Then we marched across campus to another celebration. We were being good Earth speakers! We will forever take closer looks at such things as caterpillars in the

garden. We will wonder thoughtfully when we see the long endangered species list. We are Earth Observers and these things matter to us now! We joined hands and together remembered, "I promise to be forever curious about the Earth."

- **Honoring the Earthkeeper silence tradition.** We had worked hard on becoming patient listeners. We had used a hand signal all year to call for "an Earthkeeper silence." This meant we were to raise our hand with the signal, be very still, and listen. We found there was much to be heard. We honored that time of silence now by recalling our favorite gentle earth sounds.

- **An earth biodiversity quilt.** We had studied so many wonders of the planet. We each created one block of a quilt to piece together to make an Earth quilt. We planned to put the beautiful blue Earth on a square in the center!

- **A biodiversity block game.** We had read many stories about endangered animals, such as *Will We Miss Them?* by a young girl, Alexandra Wright (Charlesbridge, 1992). Then we remembered reading *The Old Ladies Who Liked Cats* by Carol Green (HarperCollins, 1991) that, through the funny story,

helped us understand the delicate balance of nature. There is a reason for everything! On blocks we taped a small picture we had created of some important part of the earth. There were raindrops, bears, whales, an air cloud, etc. Then we carefully created a vertical standing square with the blocks, which was to represent the earth. We saw it standing firm, however, and we realized now that each square was important for the whole to survive! When we pushed one block out of the middle, the whole thing collapsed. We decided we had better protect the parts of the planet. We illustratred our experience to help us remember!

# An Earth Tea:
## A Time of Sharing

We knew now that every day is Earth Day, so we celebrated the earth with an Earth Tea. We invited our parents and performed many poems and songs paying tribute to the Earth. We recited the sad song of the last whale and we chanted the Zuni sunrise with great respect. The year had passed quickly.

During the remaining few minutes we had as first graders, we shared another story. This one was called *Wilson's World* (HarperCollins, 1971).

In the story a boy named Wilson has special paints and brushes with which he can paint his world any way he wishes it to be. The world is beautiful at first, but in time more people come building more places on the planet and the earth starts to become polluted and ugly. Before it is too late, Wilson takes his special paint and brushes and makes his world clean and beautiful again! He realizes, as we have, that if we all work together we can protect our beautiful home—the Earth. As we grow up and the issues become more complex, we will continue to make choices for the planet. We understand the earth belongs to us all!

# A Final Note:

There was no time left to write about *Wilson's World*, so Helen gave each child the opportunity to record his/her reply to the question, "If I had Wilson's special paints and brushes, how would I paint my world?" The replies were thoughtful and touching. The planet is in good hands!

*Dear Mrs. Dee: If I had some brushes and paints and could paint a picture of my world, it would be filled with clean air and lots of green grass, and people who care about the earth and animals, and laws about killing animals, and a sky all clear, and fresh air and not pollution in the water, and everybody recycling, and no more landfills, and no more factories polluting, and everyone caring about the earth. And, Mrs. Dee, we'll always remember the poem "Save the Earth" by Betty Miles:*

**People everywhere breathe the same air,
Share the same seas, live together on the land.
People everywhere, who learn, plan, work, care,
CAN SAVE THE EARTH!**

Danas Wrold is Clean

# Books for Earthkeepers

**Asch, Frank.** *The Earth and I.* Harcourt Brace & Co., San Diego, 1994.

**Aschenbrenner, Gerald.** *Jack, the Seal and the Sea.* Silver Burdett, Englewood Cliffs, New Jersey, 1988.

**Brown, Ruth.** *The World that Jack Built.* Dutton, New York, 1991.

**Cherry, Lynn.** *The Armadillo from Amarillo.* Harcourt Brace Jovanovich, San Diego, 1994.

**Cherry, Lynne.** *A River Ran Wild.* Harcourt Brace Jovanovich, New York, 1992.

**Deedy, Carmen.** *Agatha's Featherbed.* Peachtree, Atlanta, 1991.

**Durell, Ann.** *The Big Book of Our Planet.* Dutton Children's Book, New York, 1993.

**Fife, Dale H.** *The Empty Lot.* Little, Brown, Boston, 1991.

**Geraghty, Paul.** *The Hunter.* Crown, New York, 1994.

**Gantschev, Ivan.** *Two Islands.* Picture Book, New York, 1985.

**Greene, Carol.** *Rachel Carson: Friend of Nature.* Children's Press, Chicago, 1982.

**Greene, Carol.** *The Old Ladies Who Liked Cats.* HarperCollins, New York, 1991.

**Halsey, Megan.** *Three Pandas Planting.* Bradbury, New York, 1994.

**Hamanaka, Sheila.** *All the Colors of the Earth.* Morrow, New York, 1994.

**Hazen, Barbara.** *World, World, What Can I Do?* Morehouse, Wilton, Connecticut, 1991.

**Hurd, Edith Thatcher.** *Wilson's World.* HarperCollins, New York, 1971.

**Kroll, Kathleen.** *It's My Earth Too.* Doubleday, New York, 1992.

**Leedy, Loren.** *Blast Off to Earth.* Holiday House, New York, 1992.

**London, Jonathan.** *Gray Fox.* Viking, New York, 1993.

**Love, Ann and Jane Drake.** *Take Action.* World Wildlife Fund. William Morrow, New York, 1992.

**Lowery, Linda.** *Earthday.* Carolrhoda, Minneapolis, Minnesota, 1991.

**Luenn, Nancy.** *Mother Earth.* Atheneum, New York, 1992.

**McNulty, Faith.** *A Snake in the House.* Scholastic, New York, 1994.

**McVey, Vicki.** *The Sierra Club Kid's Guide to Planet Care and Repair.* Sierra Club, San Francisco, 1993.

**Morrison, Meighan.** *Long Live Earth.* Scholastic, New York, 1993.

**Rand, Gloria.** *Prince William.* Henry Holt, New York, 1992.

**Ryder, Joanne.** *My Father's Hands.* Morrow, New York, 1994.

**Sobol, Richard, and Jonah.** *Seal Journey.* Cobblehill, New York, 1993.

**Susuki, David.** *Looking at the Environment.* John, Wiley and Sons, New York, 1991.

**Ziefert, Harriet.** *Bob and Shirley: A Tale of Two Lobsters.* HarperCollins, 1991.

## AUDIOVISUAL MATERIALS

*Earth Day* (VHS). United Learning, 6633 West Howard Street, Niles, Illinois 60714.

# Books about Endangered Animals

**Allen, Judy,** *Tiger.* Candlewick, Cambridge, Massachusetts, 1992.

**Allen, Judy.** *Seal.* Candlewick, Cambridge, Massachusetts, 1993.

**Bare, Colleen.** *Never Kiss an Alligator.* Cobblehill, New York, 1989.

**Breeden, Robert.** *Animals in Danger.* National Geographic, New York, 1989.

**Burningham, John.** *Hey! Get Off Our Train.* Crown, New York, 1989.

**Cone, Molly.** *Come Back, Salmon.* Sierra Club, San Francisco, 1992.

**Da Volls, Andy,** and **Linda.** *Tano and Binti: Two Chimpanzees Return to the Wild.* Clarion, New York, 1994.

**Gelman, Rita.** *A Panda Grows Up.* Scholastic, New York, 1993.

**Gibbons, Gail.** *The Puffins Are Back.* HarperCollins, New York, 1991.

**Havill, Juanita.** *Sato and the Elephants.* Lothrop, Lee, and Shepard, New York, 1993.

**Jonas, Ann.** *Aardvarks, Disembark!.* Greenwillow, New York, 1990.

**Keller, Holly.** *Grandfather's Dream.* Greenwillow, New York, 1994.

**Kennedy, Teresa.** *Bring Back the Animals.* Amethyst Books, New York, 1991.

**London, Jonathan.** *Condor's Egg.* Chronicle, San Francisco, 1994.

**Paul, Derek.** *Baby Animals: Five Stories of Endangered Species.* Candlewick, Cambridge, 1992.

**Pollota, Jerry.** *The Extinct Alphabet Book.* Charlesbridge, Watertown, 1993.

**Raney, Ken.** *It's Probably Good Dinosaurs Are Extinct.* Simon and Schuster, New York, 1993.

**Wright, Alexander.** *Will We Miss Them?* Charlesbridge, Watertown, 1992.

## REFERENCES

**Few, Roger.** *Children's Guide to Endangered Animals.* Macmillan, New York, 1993.

**Hair, Jay D.** *Endangered Animals—A Ranger Rick Book.* National Wildlife Federation, Washington, D. C. 1989.

**Irvine, Georgeanne.** *Protecting Endangered Species.* Simon and Schuster, New York, 1990.

**Lazo, Carolyn.** *Endangered Species.* Crestwood House, New York, 1990.

**Meadows, Graham.** *Extinction Is Forever.* Rigby, Crystal Lake, 1991.

**Wheeler, Jill.** *The Animals We Live With.* Abdo and Daughters, Edina, 1990.

**Zoobooks.** *Endangered Animals.* Wildlife Education, San Diego, 1993.

## VIDEO

*Spirit of the Eagle* (VHS). Miramar, 200 Second Avenue West, Seattle, Washington 98119.

# Notes

# Notes